Daughter of the Wind

The Story of the Christian Women's Center

Sue Hulon-Palmer
with Charlotte Davis

GreenTree Publishers
www.greentreepublishers.com
Newnan, GA

Daughters of the Wind: The Story of the Christian Women's Center

Copyright © 2021 by Troy A. Hulon

All rights reserved. No part of this publication may be reproduced, stored in a retrieval system, or transmitted by any means – electronic, mechanical, photographic (photocopying), recording, or otherwise – without prior permission in writing from the author.

All Scripture quoted in this book is taken from the King James Version of the Bible.

Printed in the United States of America

ISBN-13: 978-1-944483-40-1

Greentree Publishers:
www.greentreepublishers.com

Net proceeds from the sale of this book will be used to benefit non-profit ministries.

Special Thanks

Thank you to my family and friends for the love and support throughout this journey. To Charlotte, thank you for your commitment and dedication to me and this book. Without you and your contribution, this hope and dream would never have become a reality.

DEDICATION

The wind bloweth where it listeth, and thou hearest the sound thereof, but canst not tell whence it cometh, and whither it goeth: so is every one that is born of the Spirit.
John 3:8

Many years ago, the Holy Wind of God moved through Griffin, Georgia, in an unusual way. He blew mightily across the lives of His children who would be used by Him to fulfill His purposes. This book is about those people who were chosen by God to do His work, sometimes together, sometimes alone, sometimes for years, and sometimes for only a season, but always following after His voice.

Others also were blown in by the Spirit. A few came in on a gentle breeze, just needing a bed for a night or two while traveling. Most gusted in with hurricane force, desperately trying to escape hunger, fear, and abuse. All were lost daughters looking for God's Holy Wind that could fill the empty space in their hearts.

This book is dedicated to the following:

The people of Griffin who witnessed God moving in their midst every day.

My family and friends who experienced with me a new way of walking with the Lord.

The residents of the Christian Women's Center, those Daughters of the Wind, who were receptacles for God's grace and mercy, as well as recipients of His daily supply.

The intent of this writing is to show the world what it means to move into unfamiliar territory, on paths without direction, with only a compelling Voice to follow. It is a frightening place to be, yet the fear is mitigated by the knowledge that He is a loving Father who will never forsake His children. May we never forget all that He was, all that He is, and that He is always with us!

But ye are a chosen generation, a royal priesthood, an holy nation, a peculiar people; that ye should shew forth the praises of Him who hath called you out of darkness into his marvelous light.
1 Peter 2:9

FOREWORD

I first met Sue Hulon at an annual corporate meeting in January of 1992. I was invited by a neighbor, Mace Palmer, and during dinner, she announced to everyone at our table that I would make a really good Board Member. Ignoring all my protests to the contrary, she popped right up in the business session and submitted my name. Although I did not know even one person in the entire room except Mace, when the vote was taken, I was among those elected. It was a God moment for sure and certain! The best part of that evening was meeting and getting to know Sue. Working with her as a Board Member was quite an experience. She had a way of doing whatever she felt God was calling her to do and then telling the Board about it later. Sue was much better at asking forgiveness than asking permission.

After a few years, I resigned from the Board to become Sue's secretary and later became the bookkeeper for the Center. Through all those years, Sue and I developed a lasting friendship that endures even today. Though her health is declining now, I remember clearly that feisty visionary who would say to me, "God is showing me we need to...," and she would name some project for which we had no money. I would remind her of our finances, and she would say, "If God is telling me to do it, there is money somewhere. Find it." Sure enough, the money would come in at just the right time. Her faith was amazing, as was her boldness in carrying out God's instructions in spite of any opposition she might encounter.

It was that incredible tenacity and enduring faith in God that helped Sue keep the Christian Women's Center going on more than one occasion when others might have given up. At one point, we were $40,000 behind in Thrift Store rent and other bills, but Sue never wavered in her trust that God would provide. How could God not respond to that kind of belief in His provision? Within four months, He brought in all the necessary funds and those past due bills were completely paid.

Right up to her retirement, Sue seemed to have an unending reserve of energy. She could have rivaled the Energizer bunny for stamina! She never tired of providing a place of safety for the women who needed the Center's services.

This book chronicles how God tamed the wild child and harnessed all that rebellion for His purposes. Then He called Sue and the women in her circle of influence to provide a refuge for those around them who had no way to escape from the crises they were facing in their lives. As you read this miraculous story of the Holy Spirit working through a group of ordinary housewives, you should know without a doubt that He can use anyone who will hear and follow His voice.

Charlotte Davis

TABLE OF
CONTENTS

Chapter 1

The Early Years

To every thing there is a season, and a time to
every purpose under the heaven....
a time to plant, and a time to pluck up
that which is planted.
Ecclesiastes 3:1-2

In 1983, God moved powerfully into our
town of Griffin, Georgia. Yes, of course, He was
already there, and yes, He had moved powerfully before, but I don't think He had ever done
anything quite so radically different. I don't
know why Griffin, I don't know why me, and I
don't know why He chose the particular people
He did to carry out the work. I do know the
movement of God's Spirit was so significant
that our entire community was impacted. He
unified all denominations in every economic
level, enabling them to work together in peace.
From the very beginning, the only possible explanation was that God was moving among all
the people involved.

When I think back, I wonder when it was
that God really began to work in my life. Was it

before I was born? Was it as a child in a Methodist Sunday School class? Or was it as a teenager, dragged to church by my mother and aunt and made to sit under God's Word whether I wanted to or not? Perhaps it was a combination of all of those influences together, but they culminated in a meeting with God on a Baptist pew one Sunday morning in Morrow, Georgia.

Anyone who knew me as a teenager would certainly have wondered how I got to that Baptist pew in the first place. My parents loved me but didn't quite know what to do with this wild girl-child who had such a strong, rebellious streak. I was bent on doing whatever I wanted to do with no thought of the consequences of my actions.

> "The movement of God's Spirit was so significant that our entire community was impacted."

Eventually, I began sneaking out at night to meet a young man of whom my parents disapproved. Being unable to prevent my nighttime escapades, my father took a drastic step: he moved us from the Griffin area to Forest Park, Georgia.

The change of scenery did have the desired effect of dampening my infatuation with the young man in question, but it did not quell my rebellion in any way. I just made new girl-friends and then sneaked out to be with them and their young men. The choices I made created continuous conflict at home and we were all unhappy. I was looking for a way out from under the constant restriction my parents represented.

On one of my trips out the bedroom window, my girlfriends and I went to the drugstore on Ponce de Leon Avenue in Atlanta, a destination that would have brought great consternation to my mother had she known where I was headed. The girls had set me up with a blind date that night whose name was Donald Hulon. All my friends went off with their guys on motorcycles, but Donald had a big, fancy, red car, and I was impressed. I was even more impressed with the kiss he stole before we even left the drugstore parking lot!

Donald and I began to see each other on a regular basis, and eventually he provided the escape I wanted. Donald's grandmother owned a huge house near Grant Park, and she rented out rooms. While we were dating, we were in and out of her house often, and I liked her a lot. One night, after a particularly nasty argument with my parents, I called Donald, said I was leaving, and asked him to please come get me. He picked me up and took me to his grandmother's house. She was happy to give me a place to stay in order to keep me off the streets.

By this time, Donald was ready for me to be his and his alone, but I was unwilling for anyone to put limitations on my new-found freedom. I got a job at a carwash in downtown Atlanta that allowed me to move away from him and what I considered to be just another person trying to control me.

The answer I needed came in the form of a shared apartment on Ponce de Leon Avenue near Emory with a girl from the Vaughn Community in Spalding County. I felt certain that someone from my childhood hometown could surely be trusted. That assumption turned out to be false because one day she vanished with all of our rent money and half of my clothes. That situation brought a sudden end to my burst of independence and forced me to return home to Mom and Dad whether I liked it or not. Thank God, they were willing to take me back into their home.

Submitting to my parent's authority was still an issue for me, so when I got an opportunity to live with my grandmother in Alabama, I jumped at the chance. She was a godly woman who knew the source of her strength. In any crisis, you could find her on her knees in her prayer closet— literally in a closet! I am convinced that it was the covering of her prayers that protected me through all my rebellious years. It took a STRONG angel to keep me out of the gutter during that time because when there was a choice to be made, I picked the gutter every time. My mother was once told by one of my teachers that I would always be a C and D student, never accomplishing anything in my life, but she didn't know I had a secret weapon - a praying grandmother.

Eventually, the lack of action in Alabama drove me back to Georgia. The party girl could not exist without a party. Not long after my return, Donald called to notify me that he had listed me as his wife on an insurance form so that if anyone contacted me, I would give the right answer. That call put him on my radar again. Having lost touch with all my former friends and with no new connections on the horizon, Donald shot to number one on my list for a date. We began to see each other regularly, and my parents finally came around to approving him as a boyfriend. He had a job, a car, and was level-headed, all the things they thought their defiant, disobedient daughter needed in a husband. So, when Donald popped the question, they were firmly on his side and were happy to provide a "high church" wedding. As for me, being married was initially like living in fairy land. I was Donald's princess, he was my king, and we were naive enough to believe that we would live happily ever after. Boy, did we have a lot to learn!

Chapter 2

Surrender

And then will I profess unto them, I never knew you; depart from me, ye that work iniquity.
Matthew 7:23

Don't ask me how it happened, but I actually began married life with all the necessary skills to take care of my home and my new husband. Somehow, in spite of myself, Mother had managed to teach me what I needed to know, and I found that I actually liked being a wife! We bought a cute little house in Forest Park near my parents and dove into life headfirst. To make ends meet, I took in ironing and sewing and even got a job as a substitute teacher working at the school where our two children attended. My husband worked long hours, coming home late after traveling many miles.

Over time, we became friends with the people in our neighborhood. Many of them were near our age and most of us had small children. We ladies were a close group, sharing food and drinks, babysitting, and rides to the store. Life was a struggle, but the parties were great, and although Donald and I argued on a regular basis by now, we just thought that was what married people did. The years passed while we and everyone else in our group were so caught up in living each day that we had no time to think of eternity.

One particular morning, I woke with a feeling that I needed to go see one of my friends from the neighborhood, but I had things to do and ignored my intuition. Feeling justified by my long to-do list, I went on my busy way. Sadly, there was never another opportunity, for that night she had a massive stroke and the next day, she was gone.

Having grown up in a Christian home, I knew the routine for a funeral. The church would provide breakfast, coffee, and donuts, friends would also furnish food, and the family would be comforted by the outpouring of love. That is how it works in the South anyway. So, I made a covered dish and headed to her house, but the scene I walked into jarred my sensibilities.

The family was crying uncontrollably, and whiskey bottles were everywhere. The kitchen, which should have been a beehive of activity as friends served food and cleaned dishes, was dead cold. No church people arrived to help because that family, like my own, had no time for church. At her husband's request, I helped him select a suit for the funeral and then left as quickly as I could. The crying and distress of loss were unbearable. There was no hope in that house, just the wailing voices of cold death—not the coldness of the girl who had died, but the hopelessness of the ones left behind.

> "There was no hope in that house, just the wailing voices of cold death—not the coldness of the girl who had died, but the hopelessness of the ones left behind."

The day of the funeral arrived, and one of the sons was brought to the service in chains. I was shocked, thinking of the times he had played with my own children. I remember how sad I felt to hear the preacher say, "I never knew her, but I know she was nice."

Then I heard the Lord say to me as I sat on that pew, "And I don't know you," and He brought a Scripture to my mind which I now know is from Matthew 7:23: ***"I never knew you; depart from me, ye that work iniquity."***

I promised myself that day to try to go to church more often. I left the service and drove home quietly, but it wasn't long before I got back into the swing of family life, and my promise to God faded to the back of my mind.

My mother-in-law, bless her heart, had more concern for the spiritual condition of my family than I did. She arranged for my children to be picked up in front of our house by a bus, and she would meet them when they arrived at the church. Donald and I were glad, not because of what our boys would learn with her, but because it gave us some time alone together.

One morning, I was busy cleaning the kitchen while Sport and Troy were waiting for the bus, so I asked their father to watch them through the window. When I came back into the room and looked into the yard, the children were gone. I asked if they had gotten on the bus, but Donald did not know because he had been watching television. I didn't worry much until I saw the bus from his mother's church stop by our driveway, and my boys were not there to get on it. Where were my children? No one knew.

The bus driver did tell me another church bus came through our neighborhood and could have picked them up by mistake. He did not know the name of the church and suggested I wait to see if they brought my kids home before taking any other action. I was frantic, but there was little to do but wait. Sure enough, at 1:30 in the afternoon, the other bus bought them home, not even realizing the children had been lost. I thanked God profusely and promised again to go to church.

How many messages did God have to send to get my attention? Would He take my boys from me if I continued to ignore Him? I didn't know Him well enough at the time to figure that one out, but I was not taking any chances! The very next Sunday, I sent the boys to Sunday school with their grandmother, promising I would be there later for church. That is how I came to be on that Baptist pew, alone with God. I had run from Him until I was exhausted.

As I sat there, I began to pray about my marriage, my children, and all my other cares. God said, "Just give it all to me," and I did.

"Lord, I know you are my Savior. I've known that since I was a child. But I need you to take over my life. I can't do this anymore. I can't play the game."

I don't know what the sermon was about that day, but I do know that I surrendered all of me to the Lord on that bench in Morrow, Georgia....everything! I got up with nothing but a new me. In the succeeding days, I found the Word of God was easier to read, and I could understand it. I loved my husband and children with a different kind of love. Oh yes, I had the same life, but I saw it with new eyes. I was changed. I had been falling apart, but now I was at peace. How could that be? Only the Holy Spirit can make that kind of difference in a human life, and He was finally at work in mine.

Chapter 3

New Beginnings

And ye shall seek me, and find me, when ye
shall search for me with all your heart.
Jeremiah 29:13

Time stands still for no one and certainly
not for growing families. Our boys were getting
older, our house seemed to be getting smaller,
and our neighborhood was changing. Donald
and I discussed the need for getting the boys
into a different environment, but my vision
was a house with "character," one close to
good schools and malls. My husband's vision
was 180° opposite of mine. Just how different
his idea was became clear when he found a
rambling, old farmhouse on a dusty, red dirt
road in Griffin, Georgia. My life was about to
come full circle and take me back to the same
town where I had started.

Neither of us had any inkling that God was
beginning to move in our lives. I was certainly
not looking to leave my comfortable city life,
but Donald saw plenty of land where the boys
could play and turned a blind eye to all the

repairs the old house would require. He didn't even take the time to discuss the purchase with me. He simply turned to the realtor and said, "We'll take it," and I almost fainted! The house with "character" I had imagined in my designer mind turned into a constant struggle of broken pipes, paint remover, and paint. More than that, every time it rained, the yard became a morass of red mud in which my city high heels sank out of sight.

I cried and begged, all to no avail. Donald stuck to his guns and immediately implemented his plan to move the children and me, along with our loveable Basset hound, Earthquake, to Griffin. (Speaking of our pet, here is a piece of free advice: never name your dog Earthquake. If he should happen to escape from your yard, as ours did on more than one occasion, and you walk down the street yelling "Earthquake, Earthquake," I can absolutely guarantee you will create quite a stir in your neighborhood!)

"Okay," I said through my tears. "I'm a decorator. Surely I can make this work." What I wasn't counting on was the "no money" part of my plan. We were paying two house notes until the old one sold, plus we were traveling back to Forest Park every week for work and school. Although we were in Griffin only on the weekends to make repairs and put up fences, we still needed food at both houses—more expense. That meant little money was left for turning Donald's "eyesore" into my idea of a good home.

While the boys and my husband viewed our weekends as a continuing vacation, the emotional cost for me was immense. In addition to trying to fix things up on a shoestring budget, there was no washer, no dryer, and only ONE bathroom. On top of all that, Earthquake was hit by a car and killed. I didn't see how things could get any worse and had little hope they would get any better.

> "Physically, we may have been watching rain turn the Georgia clay to mud; but spiritually, I was in a dry and thirsty land."

My spiritual life was in just as much disarray as the house I was trying to make into a home. Physically, we may have been watching rain turn the Georgia clay to mud; but spiritually, I was in a dry and thirsty land. The problem was I didn't know how to find an oasis. I knew Jesus as my personal Savior, but I had begun to realize that I didn't "know" Him, at least, not with the intimate, experiential knowledge referred to in the Bible.

Searching for a closer, deeper walk with my heavenly Father, I began to read the Word regularly again and started to attend the church of my childhood, Pomona Methodist. The ladies there were my mother's long-time friends, so they all knew me. Before long, I was attending Sunday school, Bible study groups, and, of course, fund raisers and cookouts. One monkey wrench in my desire for spiritual growth was the fact that Pomona had only Sunday morning services every other Sunday and no services on Sunday or Wednesday nights. During those down times, I bounced from one church to another to hear whatever speaker was advertised or to attend whatever Bible studies they offered. I was hungry for God and didn't care which denomination offered to feed me as long as their teachers and speakers were true to the Scriptures.

Through my roaming from church to church, I began to make friends with women in the Griffin community. Before long, God impressed upon me to begin a Bible study in our home and that I was to teach it. Certainly, I had misunderstood because I could not speak in front of people and told God if I tried, I would fall on my face. He just led me to Scripture that said He would never leave me nor forsake me. His sense of humor was evident as

He made it clear to me that if I fell on my face, He would be right down there on the floor with me.

"Okay, Lord, but we are going down!" I snickered. I knew no one would come to a Bible study at an unfinished old house so far out from town, so I was safe. Well, the joke was on me because everyone I invited came! Not only did they come, but as we studied, we began to grow spiritually. I finally admitted that what was happening in my house was truly of God when we put a sheet of plywood over some blocks to make a ramp into the back door and actually rolled a piano into the house without everything crashing through.

Eventually, we fell into a pattern, meeting every Thursday morning for spiritual food and following up with lunch. We were just a group of housewives from a small town in Georgia trying to grow in grace, with no idea what God was planning to do through us.

Chapter 4

God's Boot Camp

...If any man minister, let him do it as of the
ability which God giveth.
1 Peter 4:11

Weeks flowed into months as I wrestled
with leaky faucets, rusty pipes, ripped screens,
and the myriad other things that come with
trying to modernize an old house. My family
was adjusting to our new life better than I. At
least, God had now given me sisters in Christ
to meet with every week to strengthen my
walk, and I desperately needed that strength.
As I picked up beer cans in the house and in
the yard, I would say "I can do all things
through Christ, who strengthens me. Isn't that
true, Lord?" I repeated it while I brought in
wood for the heater to warm the women who
were coming for teaching, healing, and prayer.
I said it again as I prepared the lunch I would
enjoy with my friends.

Still, I felt empty, as if something were
missing. One Thursday in our study group,
out of the blue, I opened my mouth and what
came out shocked even me. I said that I was

going into the prisons to minister. Now, I certainly didn't know how to make that happen,
and neither did anyone in my immediate circle,
but God, as always, was three steps ahead.
The very next day, an acquaintance called to
say she was working in the women's prison in
Milledgeville and asked if I would like to join
her. "God," I thought. "You sure work fast!"

Because God was obviously on the move, I
decided to just jump in with both feet. My
friend asked if I would speak to the women,
and I agreed. When she made her next trip to
Milledgeville, I went along. I was not prepared
for the feelings I experienced as we drove up to
the prison. I was a little jumpy, but only because I had never been in a women's prison
before. The rules said no guns (of course), no
jewelry, and no purses—only a driver's license
to prove identity.

As we passed the barbed and razor wire on
the fences, it hit me that we were not just driving by, but we were going inside to interact
with these women. Then, I realized that we
saw women like them every day and never paid
any attention to them to say "Hi" or "Can I
help you?"

The attendant at the gate pulled me back
to reality when she snapped, "Your driver's license," and held out her hand. She offered no

please or thank you. As I walked through the door and it clanked behind me, I cringed, knowing that we were in with no way out. It was a cold feeling, but I followed the group down the hall.

> "Where were you when I needed you? I wouldn't have killed my husband if I had heard this back then."

We were led to an auditorium with a stage, and as we entered, the cell mates joined us from side doors until the room was filled. Guards were stationed between us and them. With pounding heart and shaky knees, I gave my speech and thought the worst was over. But when we opened the floor for questions, one of the women stood up. She looked me straight in the eye and said, "Where were you when I needed you? I wouldn't have killed my husband if I had heard this back then."

I replied with the only answer I knew. "I'm sorry I wasn't there for you, but I have come now. I know I am too late for you and that breaks my heart. Please forgive me and our town for not helping in your time of need."

Silence filled the room, and they went out the side doors. My heart hurt for days after leaving the prison and still does to this day. I vowed right then and there I would work from that day forward to see there would be fewer women from Griffin heading to that prison, and we would work with the system to provide shelter for women coming out of that terrible place.

At the same time I was working with the women in the Milledgeville prison, I was also being drawn deeper into counseling, which is saying a lot since I had no formal training. My knowledge consisted of what I could glean from taking courses and reading everything I could get my hands on.

Then God threw me into the deep end of the pool by bringing Christy Cleghorn into my life. Exactly how we met is buried in the deep recesses of my memory. I can't remember if I first saw her at a church revival or if one of the ladies invited her to the Bible study, but I will never forget the impact she had on my life.

Christy was a red-headed, 5-foot-5 dynamo in cowboy boots. She could play the piano with such gusto that you just knew with certainty there would be "Victory in Jesus" because "The King Is Coming," (her favorite song). Because of her talent, she played for several of the churches in the area. But there was another side to Christy of which most of her Christian acquaintances were not aware. She had a drug addiction she had struggled with for many years and, of course, she had friends still caught up in that lifestyle.

One night, Christy called to say she was at the hospital with a friend who desperately needed someone to talk with and asked if I would come. I was not a licensed counselor and had no idea what to say or do, but I felt God's tug on my heart and agreed to meet them at the emergency room.

That night was the beginning of many nights of ministry, so many that the hospital staff came to know me, first by sight and then by name. During that period in Griffin's history, no formal advocacy program existed for women in the city. No one was available to respond when a rape or abuse victim or drug addict came into the emergency room. The hospital workers knew I would come, so they began to call me at the farm when needs of that type arose.

One of the women they called me to was a street person named Cara Kay who had seizures. As we got to know her a little better, she began to go to places with us. One night, she went with us to Pomona Methodist Church. In the middle of the service, I realized something was wrong and suspected a seizure was on the way. I didn't know much about her condition, but I did know the signs she was showing were not good, so we quickly got her to the pastor's office.

In a small church, the offices were usually not very big, and this one was no exception—maybe six feet by eight feet at the max. There we were, tossing about, trying to keep her from swallowing her tongue or hurting herself as she flipped and flopped under the pastor's desk. The seizure ended just about the same time as the sermon, thank goodness, so no one in the congregation even realized what had happened. Because she was rolling around on the floor while we tried to help her, we joked later about being "Holy Rollers" in a Methodist church. Holy Rollers or not, we just loved Jesus and wanted to share Him with everyone who crossed our paths.

As the weeks passed, the late-night runs to the hospital became more frequent and even extended occasionally to child abuse victims. I had a set of clothes my family called my "jump-in-and-run" clothes. They were also easy to slip out of as I crawled back into bed with my husband in the early-morning hours.

During that time, I walked among the hospital staff as they worked those midnight shifts, but I never got in the way and was careful not to overstep their authority. Thank heavens my parents' ideas about respecting limits had seeped into me even though I thought my heart was closed to their preaching. Of course, I also knew where my own boundaries were, too. I was sure of myself and didn't let others step on my lines either. We understood each other well. There were things hospital staff could not do, but they also knew I operated as a free agent and had no red tape.

> "Even the early days of rebellion and sneaking out at night were going to be used by Him as I ministered to rebellious women."

Looking back now, I can see what a tremendous learning time those days were in my life. It is amazing how much God taught me about human behavior through those wonderful nurses and doctors as well as the hurting street people I struggled to help. I didn't know it, but God was quietly laying groundwork. Even the early days of rebellion and sneaking out at night were going to be used by Him as I ministered to rebellious women. He was slowly molding and stretching me, knowing I would need those lessons later.

A big bag of quilting scraps comes to my mind as I consider those early days of my life and ministry. Every pain I suffered from bad

choices, every heart ache, and every tear were
bits and pieces of material picked up by the
Master Quilter. He just tucked them away in
the quilting bag for use later in weaving the
tapestry that He was planning for me. By January, 1983, the time appeared to be right to
send the vision that would change my life forever.

Chapter 5

The Vision

Where there is no vision,
the people perish.
Proverbs 29:18

I've heard it said before that time flies when you are having fun. I'm not sure I would have called life in an old farmhouse fun, but I had come to terms with my nemesis. Mornings had taken on a quiet rhythm as I saw my husband off to work and then settled in for some time with God before waking our boys to get dressed for school. Two cups of coffee and God's Word just before dawn were exactly what I needed to start my day. It was a practice that made every day special, and at that point, God and I had been sharing our mornings for about four years. I was learning to hear His voice in my spirit's ear and to recognize the nudging of His Holy Spirit in my daily life.

One morning, God took me into totally new territory that changed my world. As I sat quietly before the Lord that day, something began to materialize before my eyes. I wasn't sure what it was and certainly not what to call it.

Having been raised as a Methodist, I had no knowledge of visions. In our church, no one had visions; if they did, they kept it to themselves. You just didn't talk of such in a small country Methodist church! Having no frame of reference for what I was seeing, I called it a "thought pattern." It was like seeing a movie with no projector or screen. Obviously, it wasn't a dream because I wasn't sleeping. I blinked several times to make it disappear, but it was still there and not just for that day. It was with me off and on for two days.

The following Wednesday, a close friend, Brenda Hooper, came to visit, and I pounced on her as soon as she was through the door.

"Brenda, I need for you to sit down," I blurted. "I want to tell you something." Before she could even begin to formulate an answer, I started describing what I was seeing.

"I am looking up at a house with ornate iron decoration on the porch. There are people inside and a staircase leading upstairs to lots of bunk beds. I walk down the stairs into the living room where two women are sitting and talking near a cozy fireplace. One is sewing, while the other is talking to her. They are just enjoying themselves in the house. No one talks to me, but I can see myself walking among them."

"This visual thought pattern has been coming for two days. Do you think I am going crazy?" I asked with concern.

"No, I don't think you are nuts," Brenda responded, as if what I was experiencing was an everyday occurrence. Then, just as casually, she asked if I knew where the house was located.

"Yes, I think so; but I'm not going there if that is what you are thinking," I exclaimed, turning my back toward her and returning to the day's pile of laundry.

"Why?" she inquired innocently. She always acted innocent when she was planning something that would get one or both of us in trouble.

"Because I have washing, painting, and a ton of other chores to do," I replied shortly. "I am a housewife, not a flight attendant like you who has plenty of spare time. I'm not going on a wild goose chase today!" I was trying to discourage her, but my effort didn't work. Instead, she persuaded me, as all good girlfriends will do. So off we went, with Brenda driving, to discover whether or not this house really existed.

As we came into downtown Griffin and turned onto Poplar Street, there it was—exactly as I had seen it! I pointed out which house and Brenda turned into the driveway, which circled around behind the house. True to form and with no thought as to the consequences of her actions, Brenda did not stop the car until she was at the back door. We could see the house was dilapidated and needed lots of repairs.

"What are you doing?" I shouted. "Let's get out of here. Someone is going to shoot us for trespassing!" Suddenly, my heart was filled with fear. I wasn't worried so much about our physical safety as I was about how I would explain all the day's activities to my husband if he found out where I was and what I was doing. I was ready to go home right then and said so in no uncertain terms. Even my farmhouse was preferable to this one. Evidently, my panic communicated itself to Brenda. She could have rivaled racecar driver Richard Petty as she backed that car out of the driveway and sped down Poplar Street.

Chapter 6

Finding the House

"For everyone that asketh receiveth;
and he that seeketh findeth;
and to him that knocketh,
it shall be opened."
Luke 11:10

Ever have a stubborn friend who couldn't take "no" for an answer? Well, Brenda was one of those and she was not yet ready to go home, no matter what I said. Since we were in her car, I didn't have much choice. Up the street a short way lived a mutual acquaintance, Jeanette Pryor. When our hearts finally resumed their normal beating patterns, Brenda talked me into paying her a visit to see if she might know something about who owned the property. That turned out to be a "God-ordained" visit. Jeanette invited us in for coffee and a fresh cake she had just baked. She wondered aloud what had brought us to Griffin so early in the day. We gave her the short version of our story and she knew the house in question. In fact, she thought it might be

owned by her husband's company, Pryor Oil
Corporation.

"Go down to see Wallace at his office and
talk to him," she advised. We thanked her for
her hospitality and left her home with me
shaking my head in the negative. I was not in
favor of going to his office, but the chase had
already gone too far and there was no stopping
Brenda at this point. Friends will always take
you farther than you want to go and my friend
insisted we go now!

As we drove up to Pryor Oil Corporation,
Brenda said to me, "You go in and ask him. I'll
wait in the car."

"Ask him what? And why me," I demanded
in a voice which clearly indicated this had
already gone too far. "You
go in," I ordered. "This is
your crazy idea."

*"Getting out of
the car slowly, my
steps took me
toward the build-
ing like a prisoner
on the way to the
executioner."*

Brenda didn't agree
with my suggestion at all.
"You have to go. You're
the one seeing things,"
she reminded me. "Just
tell him what you saw and
ask him about the building. I'll wait here."

Her hands may not have been on my body
at that point, but she was emotionally pushing
me into the building. Getting out of the car

slowly, my steps took me toward the building like a prisoner on the way to the executioner. I expected to have to do this alone, but despite what she said, Brenda was far too curious to wait in the car. She was right behind me as I approached the receptionist's desk.

"Is Wallace Pryor in?" I asked in the best business-like voice I could muster. To my immense surprise, the receptionist showed us down the hall to his office and we introduced ourselves. Getting quickly to the point, I asked if his company owned the house on Poplar Street.

"That's a rental unit," he said thoughtfully, and I could see the curiosity in his eyes. "Why do you want to know?"

Bravely, I plunged into my story of the thought patterns, all the while expecting him to call the paddy wagon to haul us away to the funny farm. Instead, he rose from his desk and quietly offered us a seat. We listened in amazement as he began to share with us he had seen the same thing months before, but he had interpreted what he saw as a home for unwed mothers. Needless to say, I was in shock. How could he have had the same dream as I did? How could two people in two different places see the same thing months apart? With my limited experience of God at

that point in my life, I had no explanation for
what was happening.

Wallace asked if we had ever seen the inside of the house and when we said no, he offered to give us a tour. Without waiting for me
to respond, Brenda said yes immediately. We
got into our separate cars and drove up to the
house.

On the way, I worried to Brenda aloud,
"What is happening here? Where is this going? We are WAY out of control!"

We parked at the property and Wallace
chatted like we were old friends. "There are
four apartments here—two upstairs and two
down," he informed us.

We entered the building and as he spouted
all the details about the rent and utilities, I
stared in disbelief, struck suddenly by the
realness of it all. This was NOT a thought pattern. It was an old, run-down house and the
vacant apartment where we were standing was
trashed. Most of the windows were broken and
without screens, the frames were rotten, the
paint was peeling, and the door would not
even stay closed because the doorknob was
missing.

"Whoa!" I whispered to myself, trying to put
the brakes on whatever it was that was taking
place. "What am I doing? I have enough to do

at home. The last thing I need is another house to clean. This place is a wreck, and I am sure not the girl to clean up this mess!"

"Could we pray?" I quietly appealed to Brenda and Wallace, overwhelmed by what I was seeing and experiencing. I felt a sudden and desperate need to connect with my Heavenly Father.

We held hands and I spoke simply: "Lord, I don't know what is going on with what You have shown both Wallace and me, but You do. So, if this is of You, please open doors no man can close and close doors no man can open. And Lord, if You can use us for Your glory, then we give You permission. Amen."

It would be many years before I would fully realize how powerful that simple prayer really was!

Chapter 7

The Secret is Out

*Two are better than one, because they have a
good reward for their labour. For if they
fall, the one will lift up his fellow.*
Ecclesiastes 4:9-10

Some time ago, a new Christian book com-
pared following the Holy Spirit to chasing a
wild goose. In an online comment, the author
noted that while it may seem a little irreverent,
the Holy Spirit can be unpredictable, and
chasing a wild goose is certainly one way of
describing what it is like to follow Him. As we
left the rental unit and returned to Wallace's
office at Pryor Oil, I felt like a wild goose had
taken over my life, and I wasn't sure I liked it!

Wallace began to tell us total costs for utilities, and while he talked, I wondered what my
husband would think of me being in town
looking at an old house to rent on the premise
that I'd had a thought pattern. How could I
think of renting an apartment when we were
still remodeling our farmhouse, which was
costing us more than either of us had

expected? I didn't even have enough money in my pocket for a hamburger, so it was a good thing when Brenda asked if she could buy lunch. I agreed because I felt she was obligated after having been so mean by dragging me out on this wild goose chase.

A little later, Brenda took me home to my washing, cooking and everyday living, while she returned to her family and her glamorous job at Eastern Airlines. My plan was to put everything we had just seen out of my mind and pretend it never happened; but if I thought God was done with the subject, I was dead wrong. Whatever was going on in my head and before my eyes did not stop. By the following morning, the day of my weekly Bible study/ prayer group, I was still experiencing that phenomenon, and I still did not know what to call it, nor had I discussed it with my husband.

> "Have you ever belonged to a group of people who can smell a secret? They are like bloodhounds following the scent of an escaped prisoner."

As my ladies assembled on that particular morning, they immediately discerned something was peculiar. Have you ever belonged to a group of people who can smell a secret? They are like bloodhounds following the scent of an escaped prisoner. They can tell when you are hurt or in trouble, and they are hands-on people, real prayer warriors. That's how this group was, and after four years together, our hearts were so closely knit we could finish each other's sentences and thoughts. They were friends then and still are now, thirty-seven years later.

Well, on that day, I knew I needed prayer support to undertake a project of such magnitude, but I wondered if I could get by without sharing about this waking dream that kept playing in my head. No one wants her friends to think she is crazy, and I was no exception. I should have known better! If you have ever been part of a group like mine, you know that you cannot just tell them a little bit. In this case, I just casually mentioned in the conversation that I needed prayer for a house I was "seeing" downtown. From the looks on their faces, I could tell I had let the cat out of the bag, and there was NO WAY to get him back!

"Whose house?" one participant questioned.

"Where is this place?" another wanted to know.

"Are you moving?" demanded a third. "Has Donald been transferred?"

"I wish you would tell us," they all begged. "We are your friends!"

I tried valiantly to resist their pressure, but when they played the friend card, how could I say no? So, a deep breath and fifteen minutes later, they had the whole story out of me as to what I believed God was showing me. In the dead silence that followed, they just looked at me with their mouths

> "I think I have discovered why God so often begins ministries with young believers...they are too dumb to know they can't do stuff."

open, like I had three heads. Then, they erupted like volcanoes all at the same time, spewing words and questions all over me again, and I wished I had kept my mouth shut. But I could not call back the words that were already out. You just can't put toothpaste back in the tube.

As I relive those early days of preparation for ministry, I think I have discovered why God so often begins ministries with young believers who are not necessarily young in age, but young in Christ. It's because they are too dumb to know they can't do stuff. They just believe and march on. I think maybe that is where I was on that Thursday morning. After our Bible study, we decided to go out to eat downtown, but I planned to make a detour first. "You guys go ahead without me," I told them. "I'll be there a little later. I think I'm going to open an account for the house just to see what will happen."

Now, bear in mind I had no money, and it did not even cross my mind that you cannot open a checking account without some green stuff to put in it. Of course, God had it all covered. The group who thought I had lost my mind an hour ago, now wanted to be in on the action. And they intended to go with me into the lion's den, or the bank, whichever came first.

One of the ladies handed me five dollars and said, "Put this in for me."

Another said, "I'll match five dollars."

Not to be outdone, Brenda said, "Well, I can match that."

Then I remembered I had five dollars in my bank account, and I could match it, too. So, we all headed out, secure in our combined wealth, but quickly realized we had no idea which bank to use. I did know Ed Scudder, who worked at one of the banks in town, and felt confident he would help us. When we arrived, Ed graciously received us without an appointment. He and I had attended church together many years previously, so I was comfortable sharing my story with him, ending with our desire to open an account for the project to see what God had in mind.

Ed threw us a curve by wanting to know what name to put on the account. Uh, um, ah... we hadn't thought that far yet. Okay, how about we name it Hulon House because someone had said at some point over the past week that a Hulon family had lived there many years ago. How weird was that? A family I had never heard of, but who shared my surname, had lived in that very house!

"Lord," I breathed. "What are You doing?" That "out-of-control-wild-goose feeling" assaulted me again, but it was confirmation I was on the right track.

After taking our application for an account, Ed led us across the bank lobby and handed us over to a young lady who would finish up the process. He gave her our twenty dollars, and she stared at him blankly.

"It's ok," he told her quietly.

"Is there a problem?" I asked anxiously.

"Well," he replied. "It takes twenty-five dollars to open an account; but for you, we will do it for twenty dollars."

At that moment, I heard God whisper in the deep recesses of my heart, "I matched your five dollars."

"God," I thought, "You are so funny!"

As we left there, I really thought God would have a wealthy man come and give me money to buy the "Hulon House" or at least put money in the account we had just opened. Or maybe I would find a bunch of money in a bag on the street or in the woods. That was MY plan anyway, and as far as I was concerned, there was nothing more for me to do. I had done my part. Wasn't that great of me? I had made provision and could now go back to my everyday living. We had found the house, which had caused the thought pattern to stop, and an account was now open in which God could put all the money He wanted. It was for sure I would not be putting any in there. My husband didn't even know that account existed!

In fact, no one ever put any money into that checking account, other than the interest earned on the initial deposit. Many years later, we finally closed it. The lesson I learned from that experience was that God never seems to do things our way. He would use many people and bring financial support for His ministry from many different sources over the coming years, but He always moved according to His plan, not ours.

Despite the fact I was quite sure my part in whatever God was doing was completely over, God evidently did not agree. Wallace Pryor called the next morning to say he would like to make me an offer. He would pay all utilities, as well as the insurance, and would require no contract because he believed in what was happening. The rent was usually forty-five dollars a month, but he would reduce it to thirty-five dollars and then cover ten dollars of that amount from his own pocket! That would leave only twenty-five dollars a month for me to come up with.

"That is a great deal," I thanked him. "But no, I don't see how I can afford it." However, as I hung up the phone, I promised him I would pray about it. What I really meant was I needed some time to talk to my husband about what was happening, and I surely didn't feel good about doing it! Our money was short from all of the repairs and upkeep on the farmhouse. Because it was easier to speak with God than my husband, I just kept praying. I also immediately got on the phone to the women in the prayer group about the cost of Wallace's proposal.

"Well," one of my friends offered, "I can give you five dollars every month for six months out of my grocery money. My family will just give up peanut butter and see what God is up to."

Then four other women promised to give up something from their grocery list to be able to contribute $5 to the rent money. By Friday night, less than one week from the day the vision started, the rent was covered; but I still had the bridge to cross with my husband. What was I to say to him? That I was about to rent a house downtown? That very night, as we were talking, the time seemed right, and I told Donald everything. Surprisingly, he said he didn't care. As long as I was not using our money, we could do whatever we wanted. He was so overwhelmed with the farm, I'm not sure he even fully heard what I said, or maybe it was God's amazing grace covering me!

Chapter 8

Working Without a Net

*Now the just shall live by faith: but if any
man draw back, my soul shall
have no pleasure in him.*
Hebrews 10:38

Have you ever known God was on the
phone to your heart, but you were afraid to
answer the call? That's how I felt about the
whirlwind in which I suddenly found myself.
Pondering on how busy the Lord had been in
the last few days, I took inventory of all He had
accomplished in spite of my reluctance: He
had given me a visual picture in my mind; I
had seen the house; I had the promise of rent,
utilities, and insurance being provided; and
now I even had my husband's approval to
launch the project. Still, I was so unsettled in
my spirit that I could not bring myself to call
Wallace Pryor and commit. I felt like I was putting a puzzle together and did not yet have all
of the pieces. My friends used to say that God
could tell me something, but then He would
have to send me 5,000 telegrams and write it

in the sky before I would move on it. What I didn't realize was that God had the final puzzle piece and was about to put it into my hands.

On Saturday night, Dr. Mark Rutland, a former Methodist pastor who was now an evangelistic missionary, was speaking on the north side of Atlanta. Tom and Mace Palmer, along with George and Bertha Farrah, were going to hear him. Mace, who was a member of my ladies' prayer group, invited me to go along. The weather was terrible, and the forecast was even worse, so I felt sure my husband would not want me to go. But Donald and some friends were grilling out at the bar-be-que pit and having fun. He seemed not to notice the rain was getting heavier, and even with a possibility of snow before morning, he didn't mind if I went to Atlanta.

> "Have you ever known that God was on the phone to your heart, but you were afraid to answer the call?"

Getting to the Methodist church where Dr. Rutland was speaking seemed a very long drive, and it was; but as Mark began to preach, all travel weariness left me. He began to talk of God telling him to go to Africa, a place where he had never been. He spoke of suddenly having a vision, explaining that he saw himself coming off an airplane and a man being there to greet him.

As Mark related what had happened to him, I knew it was similar to what I had experienced in the way it came, the way it stayed, the lack of information. It was the same! What I had called a thought pattern, he was calling a vision. I still didn't fully understand, but I knew enough to know I'd had one.

Mark's story was not over. He continued to tell us he had acted on his vision. With no plans and very little money, he followed the Lord's direction, got on a plane, and flew to Africa. When he landed, an African man was standing there to greet him and asked if he was Reverend Mark Rutland. God had told that man to go to the airport to meet a man from the USA who was coming to preach to his people. After hearing that sermon, I never again called my experience a thought pattern. I knew I'd had a vision from God.

When we came out of the meeting, the rain had changed to snow, and it was already accumulating on the vehicles and roadways. The men were concerned we wouldn't get home safely, but I knew we would. We had been sent there so I could hear from a man of God who had seen a vision. The Lord had me on a mission, and I wasn't sure where I was going, but He was.

I felt confident the plan didn't include my going to heaven just yet. I was quiet all the way back, not because of worry, but because I was talking to God about what He had just shown me.

Needing some time alone with Jesus before waking the boys to get ready for church, I was up early the next morning. I sat in my upstairs window with my coffee, looking out and mulling over all that had happened in such a short time. There were squirrels on our property, and as I watched quietly, one of them jumped from one small limb to another. I wondered how that could be, for he was heavier than those small branches. He moved with such grace, leaping from one branch to another without a net or fear.

"How Lord?" I asked curiously.

The Lord spoke to my heart, "He was made to move in that manner."

"Lord, if that is supposed to be a lesson for me, I don't feel much like jumping. I feel more like hugging the tree or staying on a big limb. My problem is that I've already told people about this vision You've given me. Well.... maybe I could just say I ate some pizza that disagreed with me and caused me to dream strange dreams. But Lord, You and I know that isn't true. You started this wild goose chase, so now just give me the confidence to fly as You are calling me to do, even as I see Your beautiful squirrel doing. Holy Spirit, Wind of God, help me fly where You want me to, not thinking about the lack of a net, but just knowing You are always there to keep me aloft."

On Monday morning, I called Wallace Pryor to give him my decision and arrange to pick up the key to Hulon House. The following Thursday, our prayer group began with the news that my husband had given his approval and the apartment was rented. In addition to securing their help with the cleaning, I asked them to pray for guidance as to how we should proceed. We all reaffirmed our promise to fast $5 a month from our grocery money for six months to pay the rent and see what would happen. We were excited and decided to move the Bible study down to the apartment right away in hopes that we would get women from

> *"Holy Spirit, Wind of God, help me fly where You want me to, not thinking about the lack of a net, but just knowing that You are always there to keep me aloft."*

the community to come participate, if not for the study time, at least for the lunch we would provide.

We were just the naive Church, stepping out onto the streets. If God had shown us everything we would come up against, we probably wouldn't have gone outside our doors. We would have said we were not qualified, but God used what we did know and trained us fast on the street while we sang "I have decided to follow Jesus; no turning back, no turning back."

Chapter 9
Into Enemy Territory

*Have not I commanded thee? Be strong
and of good courage; be not afraid,
neither be thou dismayed: for
the Lord thy God is with thee
whithersoever thou goest.*
Joshua 1:9

The thought pattern had stopped, and I was at peace. I'm sorry. I should have said vision, for I now understood the terminology for what God had shown me. Even now, all these years later, it is hard for me to conceive that God would use such a small group of women with so little knowledge of religious affairs to begin a women's ministry in an old, dilapidated house in downtown Griffin. Yet, there we were, barreling forward at ninety miles an hour in the freezing weather.

As planned, we moved the Bible study from the farm on Steele Road to 738 West Poplar Street with our faith and our six-month commitment to each other: following Jesus - no turning back. We called the weekly meeting "Faith, Hope, and Love Bible Study." Our plan was to hold Bible studies every Thursday and then feed everyone lunch afterwards. Of course, clean-up would have to come first, and we had little money for supplies. Not to worry, God had that issue under control, too. We picked up donations here and there from women we knew because they wanted to be a part of what God was doing, and they could see Him already moving and opening doors for the ministry. We were all amazed at how God was working before our eyes.

Our core group was few in number, but enough to do what God had in mind: Brenda Hooper, Jeanette Pryor, Inez Stewart, Martha Rawdin, Mace Palmer, Bertha Westley, Christy Cleghorn, LaVerne Smith (my mother), and myself. As often happens in a Georgia winter, the weather had turned pretty, and we had worked really hard in the yard. We were now ready to announce ourselves to the community, so I called a sign maker in town, Robert Presley, for a sign to be put in our clean front yard.

We were looking forward to the luncheons and Bible studies we would hold, so next we tackled the house, cleaning it as best we could. At one point, I remember Brenda hugging and cleaning a commode as she asked innocently, "When will the church folks get here to help us, Sue?" We all got a chuckle out of her sarcasm. Interestingly enough, it was during this time I ran into my first problem with inventory, and it was related to that bathroom: we couldn't seem to keep toilet paper in the house. I never knew how hard it was to keep a bunch of women supplied with toilet paper! I brought it from home, and so did the other women, but there never seemed to be enough.

By this time, it was obvious we needed some financial assistance, so we decided to have a yard sale in the early spring to help with expenses. Mother and Mrs. Bertha were all for that and promised to bring in help from their respective churches. We all remembered Brenda's comment about the church folks coming to help and knew we needed them. This project was bigger than a few women could handle.

Many, like Janis Shapiro, did come to help. Janis had cerebral palsy, and her bones were as twisted as a grape vine, but she never complained. One day, she had been working in the living room when she spotted a coat hanger under the couch. She somehow managed to prod, poke, and grab that coat hanger from behind the couch before the rest of us could blink an eye. We were all amazed and ashamed at how much work she did with her poor health and twisted body. Later, Janis became a dedicated member of our Board of Directors until her declining health forced her to resign.

People came for different reasons, with different motives, and at different times, but always with a desire to work for God. I was amazed, and still am, at how and why they came. It wasn't because I asked them because I didn't know most of them at that time in my life. It was simply that the Lord was always placing the right person in the right place at the right time. It was funny to watch and hear their stories of how they arrived. Most were dragged in by a friend and some by God, Himself.

As I write this story, I am humbled by the many people the Lord sent. Over and over, I told people it was God, not me, issuing invitations to be a part of the ministry. They really had trouble believing God could move the women of a city to provide food and shelter for a large number of residents without being poked and prodded the way Janis did

> "We were all believers, but we were experiencing God personally in a way that we never had before, and it strengthened our faith."

that coat hanger. Yet move them He did, and they continued to come.

We were all believers, but we were experiencing God personally in a way we never had before, and it strengthened our faith. We took that strong faith back into our families and it made a difference in our lives and in the world around us. We were charting new territory and did not even know from week to week if we would be able to continue. Yet, whatever the need, God seemed to have someone in mind.

For example, word had traveled by then the kitchen was in dire need of a "do-over," and a group of women showed up to paint the kitchen and spruce it up a little. By this time, my plate was full with the women's prison and ministering at the hospital, as well as getting the house off the ground, so I had no time to worry about the kitchen. I told them to go to it, and they did! When Nancy Murray's group got through with that kitchen, it sported white cabinets with big red hearts on them, so every woman who entered there knew she was loved. It was the most uplifting thing we had done to that point. The house just seemed to come alive with the love of God. It was such a move of compassion that we felt we were officially in a home after that. It was a joy to have our

Thursday Bible studies and women's luncheons there.

We invited people from the neighborhood, but they were not yet quite ready to receive us. However, we did pick up a few extra people who came for the workdays and stayed for lunch to talk about what God was doing. We continued to hand out literature anyway because we had faith that we were following God's plan, even though our finances didn't show it. We just knew we needed to keep moving: no turning back, no turning back. Well, at least for six months.

Chapter 10
Officiully Official

*Where no counsel is, the people
fall: but in the multitude of
counsellors, there is safety.*
Proverbs 11:14

Six months was the amount of time we had
committed to stick with my vision. Yet we were
barely into the journey, and I was already feeling strongly that we needed to be operating
under some form of authority. I had no idea
where to turn for advice on the subject, but
our church seemed like a good starting point.
Our problem was how to approach the pastor
of a small-town Methodist church and ask for
her guidance in pursuing a vision. Not knowing what kind of response to expect, we
worked up our courage and presented our story to the pastor. Fortunately for us, she did
not faint, nor did she accuse us of heresy. In
fact, the advice we got from her was sound; we
needed to form a Board of Directors to bc effec-
tive.

"How do I do that?" I asked.

"Make a list of people you would like to help you in ministry," she replied. "Go visit each one personally and ask them to serve on your Board. If the answer is no, ask if they can recommend someone else. Then, repeat the process until you get the names of people willing to serve."

So, we began our search, and soon, I had my list. We called a meeting to elect the Board of Directors who had agreed to oversee the ministry. The following fourteen people were chosen by God to birth His new ministry: Franklin Allen, Harold Arledge, Sam Bunn, Christy Cleghorn, Tom Hunt, Lisa Jenkins, James Johnston, Barbara Keith, Wallace Pryor, Martha Rawdin, La Verne Smith, Bill Wesley, Mike Wiley, and Helen Wiley. We agreed to meet every three months since we didn't have much to vote on, but that changed quickly, and we soon were meeting monthly.

At this point, I was still making runs to the hospital on a regular basis when raped or battered women arrived there. It was pure joy for me to be able to talk about the Lord with

> "It was pure joy for me to be able to talk about the Lord with those women and tell them they could have a better life."

those women and tell them they could have a better life. After a time, I appealed to the hospital for a room in which to store clothing and to counsel with the women. We needed a quiet place to meet with a social worker or just to wait until whoever had caused the injuries was no longer lurking in the parking lot. The administration saw the need and responded quickly. Soon we were operating a rape crisis center from that room to meet this unserved need in the city.

Eventually, people began to take notice that someone with no training or credentials was filling a need that the social service organizations in Griffin were ignoring. Pressure began to build, and to their credit, the local agencies finally responded. As for me, I was glad to relinquish those midnight runs to the hospital and allow legitimate social organizations to take over the responsibility.

One of the lasting benefits of that time of ministry in the hospital was that I became familiar with the court system in Griffin and learned about rape kits and correct court procedures. I came to know the judges and attorneys in the area, many of whom became long-time friends to me and the ministry. One in particular, Trey Howell, became a volunteer advocate for the ladies, taking time to talk with them about options available then and in the future. He was one of many knights in shining armor the Lord sent our way.

Another attorney who provided a tremendous service to us was Jim Hendrix of Zebulon, GA. His advice and assistance were invaluable as we struggled to incorporate the ministry and obtain tax exempt status. Early on, we had received a strong suggestion to incorporate as protection for our Board, volunteers, and future employees. Jim agreed to guide us through the LONG and complicated process. It would be almost a year before all that paperwork could be completed and approved. When the state was satisfied we had jumped through all of their hoops, the ministry would have a new name: The Christian Women's Center. But that would happen in November and we were currently in February. At this point, we were still meeting needs on Poplar Street from a building simply known as Hulon House.

With a Board of Directors in place to help with administrative tasks and having passed the hospital counseling on to the proper social agencies, I was now able to focus my attention solely on the house that could provide shelter for women in need. We picked up a few volunteers here and there, but it appeared to me that many people (my husband included) had adopted a "wait and see" attitude. Rather than say something negative and make waves, they decided to stand back and watch, expecting everything to fizzle on its own. They thought if they didn't help us, we would lose our passion and quit. Maybe some of them just didn't know how to help and didn't want to take a chance on asking what might appear as dumb questions. It didn't matter to me. I just put my name and phone number on the door so women in need could reach me and left to do my housework. I was committed to following God's call, but I also had a family to attend.

Chapter 11

Blown in with the Snow

*But Jesus said, Suffer little children,
and forbid them not to come
unto me: for of such is the
kingdom of heaven.
Matthew 19:14*

March came, but instead of spring, we got more winter weather. The house was cold with icy drafts coming from every corner, and a space heater was our only heat. We closed the doors to the rest of the house by leaning chairs or covered bricks up against them and placed rolled rugs and towels at the bottom of the doors to block the wind. The situation was beginning to test our faith, but we persevered in prayer and marched on through Romans in our Bible study. It wasn't long before I began thinking, "What am I doing down here when I could be home in my own kitchen or by the fireplace, wrapped in my afghan. What is going on here, Lord? I'm teaching, yes, but it's cold, and no one new is coming. I don't even want to come out in this weather myself."

Still, we continued with our Bible study and serving lunch. No woman wants to eat in a cold kitchen, so a table was set up in the living room, and the luncheon was moved to a better climate. Somehow, we managed to stay warm, fellowshipping with each other and growing stronger in the Lord. We said to ourselves this neighborhood was our mission field, and we had not yet suffered unto blood.

> "We said to ourselves that this neighborhood was our mission field, and we had not yet suffered unto blood."

The cold weather was not all that tested our resolve that first winter. From mid-February to late March, we experienced snow after snow. At one point, 7.9 inches of snow was reported by the National Weather Service to have fallen at the Hartsfield International Airport in one day. We took pictures and learned a lesson on how God uses even the difficult circumstances in our lives to bring about His will.

While snapping photos of the snow, we got to talk to the children of the neighborhood. They were out of school because of the weather. Some of our group played with them in the snow until we knew their little hands were nearly frozen. We invited the children in to warm their hands and gave them the food and drinks left over from our luncheon. It wasn't much, but it gave them a glimpse of what the weird ladies in the house on Poplar Street had to offer.

One day, we saw the children coming from school, and they appeared to have no particular place to go. We decided to ask them to come in for hot chocolate, popcorn, and a Bible story. Because of our snow days together, they were not afraid and responded positively to a suggestion that they get their friends and come back every week on Thursday. Since that was the day of our Bible study, and we were already there, we would just stay later. Sure enough, they came the next Thursday with their friends.

I started out with what I thought was an easy question: "Who has a favorite Bible story?" Total silence followed, but I could see them thinking.

"Oh, come on," I said. "Someone knows just one."

Still nothing. I was amazed. So, I asked again, "What is your favorite Bible story?"

No answer! How could this be? I asked, "Haven't any of you been to Vacation Bible School and heard a Bible story?"

Finally, one little boy raised his hand and said, "What about the one where the little baby was put in the lake?"

I began with Moses, but not without first pausing to understand the moment in which I found myself. I was not from an affluent family, but I could see how blessed I was to have had an aunt and mother to take me to church. Sometimes my feet were bare, but I was taught the Word of God at Pomona Methodist Church and Sunnyside Methodist Church. I am so grateful for the time and Bible knowledge invested in me by Mrs. Penny Kilgore and a host of other godly teachers in Sunday school and Vacation Bible School over the years.

The children came slowly at first, and we sat with them and talked about the Lord in the living room in cold weather or on the porch as winter finally gave way to pretty, early spring days. I was determined the next time someone asked them to name a favorite Bible story, they would have an answer.

One of our ladies asked, "Do you think we will get in trouble with their moms?" Good question. The next time the children came, I told them to tell their mothers where they were, and parents were welcome to come every Thursday when we were there for Bible study. Eventually, one of the mothers came to see what we were doing with their children. Word spread, and some of them did come occasionally to share lunch with us.

Repairs still needed to be done on the apartment, but those children did not care that no knob was on the door. We still propped the door closed with a chair and went on, glad for the opportunity to minister to those little ones.

That winter of 1983 was cold, windy and wet. At home, I couldn't paint because of the rain and snow, but I could teach, so off I went to the house and children every chance I got. Again, we saw God demonstrate His faithfulness. When the children began to come, He sent women to work with them, and I was really glad for the help. It was as if the winter wind blew in to clear the way for the children's ministry. We didn't plan it; they drifted in with the snow. It was just another one of those things that God did. But now I had a bigger problem than toilet paper. "Where will I put them all, God?" I asked. "We need more room!"

Chapter 12
Growing Pains

*For precept must be upon precept,
precept upon precept; line upon
line, line upon line; here a
little and there a little.
Isaiah 28:10*

Sometimes, while writing this missive, I see my audacity and am amazed at myself, but I knew God walked with me, and I had no doubt or fear. He was answering the prayer I had prayed at the very beginning, standing in the apartment with Brenda and Wallace Pryor. He was opening doors no man could close and closing doors I could not open when I was going the wrong way.

The need for more space created one of those open doors. I looked day after day at the apartment adjacent to ours. It was not rented, just sitting there unused. One day, we took the bull by the horns, cleaned it up, and then began to pray over the people who would rent it. No one came, and we decided to take the land, quietly moving into it little by little. We continued to pray daily for the people who would eventually live there, but in the meantime, there was no reason to let it sit there empty. Finally, I called Wallace Pryor to ask if we could use the area until he rented it, or I could get the money for it, whichever came first. I also asked if he would give me the same deal on the second apartment as he had on the first. He agreed if we would allow his Full Gospel Men's group to meet weekly in the front room of the first apartment. They had been meeting in their homes and the wives were beginning to complain. We quickly agreed because no one was in the house at night or on weekends anyway, at least, not at that time.

Now we found ourselves with access to two apartments: one for luncheons and Bible study and one for the children and a small office. With extra space to accommodate all the children, we began to raise funds from people who were interested in seeing a children's ministry established in downtown Griffin. The donations were not large—five dollars here and five dollars there—but the growth was fast and phenomenal. I couldn't believe it!

The office was really a closed-in porch, but it gave me a separate space I could use for talking with women who had been battered or raped. We also used it to store pamphlets and clothing. It could be accessed through the porch door which allowed me to come and go without disturbing those in the house. To call that area an office might be stretching things a bit because there was no office furniture or equipment. But in Romans 4:17, the Bible says God *"calleth those things which be not as though they were."* Expecting God to provide, we called it an office, and He began to respond in that area as well. Before long, a copy machine was donated, and we thought we were in high cotton. It was really a duplicating machine; the kind with the barrel in the middle where the ink was poured into it. Yes, we got it all over us just like everyone else who ever used one, but we were happy for such a wonderful blessing. In an office with no supplies, anything is welcome.

I found myself picking up gym clips I saw on the ground and taking them back to the office. It wasn't long before that habit caught on and everyone saved gym clips and rubber bands, for we didn't have an office account to draw on. About the only thing we did have was a desk phone (paid for with money from a church donation), so our families could get in touch with us if needed. Remember, this was in an era before cell phones.

Often in ministry, there never seems to be enough of anything, yet miraculously, there somehow is enough of everything. There was always just enough food, just enough toilet paper, and just enough money. More im-

> "Often in ministry, there never seems to be enough of anything, yet miraculously, there somehow is enough of everything."

portantly, the right people always showed up at just the right time. At that point in our ministry, God sent a family of angels to help us minister. Richard and Connie Broom with their sons, Chris and Casie, began to volunteer. Connie became our secretary and put a lot of things on paper for us. Had it not been for her in the early days, no written records would exist because stopping to write stuff down is not my strong suit. Connie held down the fort in the office and helped tend the women who came in. I did the speaking and teaching, while caring for my family. Richard and the boys, along with other volunteers, taught the children. We had our hands full!

Women of the community, like Alice Garrison and Sue Savage, saw the need and came to help. Sue was convinced that even though we were a ministry, we were also a business and as such, needed to be a member of the Chamber of Commerce. She felt so strongly about the Chamber membership that she paid the dues every year until she left this earth many years later.

As far as the government was concerned, I had no idea where to go or what to do. I didn't know who was who or who had issues with whom. I went in like a bull in a china shop. I just wanted to get the job done for women and keep them safe. Sue helped me navigate through the waters of the civil and political scene in Griffin. I became a warrior in prayer for those hurting women in our city, and Sue helped by standing behind me all the way in the community.

Another pair who met a great need for us were Mike and Helen Wiley. They were members of our Board of Directors, and at meetings, they had heard the litany of all the things at the house needing repair, with no money to pay for any of it. One day, they showed up with Mike's little toolbox and came to our rescue with their great big smiles. That was the first of many visits as Mike fixed broken windows, broken doors, broken bathrooms, and anything else we could find that needed a repairman's touch. He laughingly told us he had the longest "honey-do" list in all of Griffin. What a blessing they were!

What a wonderful day for us when we had a door that would close and lock. It was such a simple thing, but major for us because now we were able to protect our belongings, as well as the people who would eventually come there to stay. "That's one more step forward. We're getting there, little by little. Thank you, Lord!"

Chapter 13

Conflict Arises

*Be sober, be vigilant; because your
adversary the devil, as a roaring
lion, walketh about, seeking
whom he may devour.*
1 Peter 5:8

Everyone knows that when you step into
the devil's territory to reclaim souls, you will
get some blowback from him. Things had been
going really well with the house, the children,
and the volunteers, so I was expecting to be
attacked in some way. What I did not expect
was it would come from within our core group
and on a day we, as Methodists, considered to
be particularly special in the week before
Easter.

It was March 31, 1983, Maundy Thursday.
If you don't know the meaning of that day, it is
the Thursday before Easter Sunday, and tradi-
tion says Christ would have celebrated the
Passover with his disciples on that day. It was
also the day He washed their feet. Early on in
our little group, we had wondered what it
would be like to have a foot washing and had

decided to follow the example Jesus had set on that night so long ago. Four years later, we were still participating in that ritual every year before Easter, only this year, we planned to do it at the house on Poplar Street.

A local pastor came and gave us commun-ion, and we began our worship time, only to be rudely interrupted by one of our group who was not in attendance. There had been some controversy with her. I can't even remember what it was at this

> "When you step into the devil's territory to reclaim souls, you will get some blowback from him."

point, but she was upset with me. I thought we had settled our differences, but evidently not. As we were pouring water, washing feet, and singing praise songs, we heard an old truck park in the driveway and heard the driver race the motor several times. Then, she burst through the door and began to remove from the house everything she had donated. One of the women at the meeting jokingly said, "Hurry and pass me the bucket before she takes that too!"

We just ignored her, hoping that once she got all her things out, she would be satisfied and leave. Well, that was wishful thinking.

She sat herself down and waited until the class was over. Then she told me she wanted all the money back her mother had donated to the ministry.

I said, "No, I don't think that is what your mother would want, but I will call her and ask. If that is her wish, I will give it to you." So, I called her mother, who had been our very first donor, and explained what was about to happen to her donation.

The mother's response was swift and loud. "Hell no!" she yelled into the phone. "I gave that money to the ministry, and I want it to stay in the ministry. Do not give my daughter any of it."

I repeated what she had said to her daughter and turned to go back to the luncheon, but she came after me saying, "I will break every bone in your skinny little body!"

It was obvious she was not calming down and was upsetting the house, so I headed out to my car to leave. She followed me onto the porch and was making a scene for all of Poplar Street to see. I just got into my car and drove to Hanleiter Methodist Church, where I found my way to the altar. My plan was to stay there with my Lord until things cooled down.

"Lord," I prayed, "What am I to do when Christian people come against me? Why is she so angry with me? She is my friend. I don't like being a leader if it puts me at odds with my friends. I want to quit!"

And I did want to quit, but I had experienced that feeling many times in the few months since the vision had pushed me into this wild goose chase. I stayed on my knees at the altar for the rest of the afternoon, asking

> "I don't like being a leader if it puts me at odds with my friends. I want to quit!"

the Lord to help me understand how to deal with the situation and others I would come up against. When I returned, my angry friend was gone. The girls in the study group said she settled down after I left and became peaceful. In fact, she got over her problem with me and was involved in the ministry for many years after, even serving as a member of the Board of Directors for a time. As for me, I went back to doing what God had called me to do, but I found I had to run away every few days and find an altar to pray.

April came and finally brought the warm weather we craved. With money so scarce, it was time for the yard sale we had discussed a few months earlier. We picked a bright, sunny day to set up our chairs and spread out our goods. There were no funds for an ad in the paper, but word-of-mouth worked for us and the yard sale was a great success. During the sale, we bought drinks and Krystal hamburgers from the proceeds. Someone called us to accountability, pointing out that all income needed to go into a checking account before being spent, so then everyone had to ante up and put back what we had used.

Up until this point, the little money we had was kept in a cigar box, along with receipts for expenses. Now, we had the yard sale money and were beginning to pick up a few more donations here and there, which meant we needed to be more careful to avoid any appearance of mishandling finances. So off to the bank we went, and I opened THREE checking accounts: a "yellow" account for income, a "blue" account for the household expenses, and a "green" account for major expenses. It sounds crazy, but with no financial background, it was the only way I could keep up with the income and outgo. "Okay, Lord," I whispered under my breath, "Don't give up on me. I'm learning!"

It was obvious we needed someone other than me to handle what little income we had. Suan Hunt was a good friend of mine and a wonderful person as well. She was smart and honest, and I knew she could keep us straight.

With pleading, puppy-dog eyes, I told Suan things were piling up on me, and I couldn't do everything. With a straight face and pure heart, I said the job would not entail much work, mostly just a few receipts in an old cigar box. When I finally got around to telling her about the three checking accounts, I reminded her that even with multiple accounts, there wasn't much money to go in them.

Suan rolled her eyes at me, but reluctantly agreed to take on the task, thinking it would not be much money at all—maybe a dollar here and a dollar there. I said again, "We only get a few donations for rent and the little bit that comes in from occasional yard sales. It will be simple because we are a small ministry." Well, Suan took the job and later she would recount with amazement how we grew and grew and grew. Over time, she saw firsthand how God met our needs, and occasionally our wants, on a daily basis. One particularly touching story was of a little boy who came with his mother to Hulon House seeking shelter from a traumatic situation in their lives. With all his heart, he wanted macaroni and cheese. His mother told him there was no money to purchase any, and he would have to do without. But she told him he could pray and ask God to give him some.

The next day, while that little one was at school, a case of mac and cheese was donated! We spread the boxes onto his bed and then told him when he came home that he had to go straight to his room. He thought he was in trouble and balked, but his mom insisted he go. When he walked into the room, his eyes widened to enormous proportions. Then he just jumped into the middle of the bed and rolled among the boxes. He wanted to eat it all for supper. A few days later, when he and his mom left us, all that macaroni and cheese went home with him.

Over time, seasons of ministry will sometimes change, and that change happened for Suan. Eventually, she was needed in other places of service, but as usual, God was ready ahead of time with another person to step into her shoes. Over the years, He sent many qualified women to handle the money, eventually allowing us the financial stability to create a paid position. Carolyn Baker came along after Suan, followed by Barbara Keith and a whole string of other women dedicated to serving the Lord by keeping the ministry's finances and me in good order. All of those wonderful women of God were blessed to witness Him moving the hearts of people to provide money (and macaroni) exactly when we needed it. Wow!

How awesome to see the miracles happen as God grew what was in that small cigar box to meet the needs of women and children in crisis every day.

Suan and I have often laughed over how I roped her into that job. Before she left, she and her husband, Tom, donated a beautiful piece of framed stained-glass to hang in the entry hall of the Center in memory of her time with us. She still tells the story of my insisting to her it would only be a few dollars here and there, mostly just a few receipts in an old cigar box. I guess sometimes I lie and don't even know it!

Chapter 14

The First Resident

*It is of the Lord's mercies that we are
not consumed, because His
compassions fail not. They
are new every morning:
great is Thy faithfulness.
Lamentations 3:22-23*

Remember how my friends said God would
have to send me 5,000 telegrams or write His
instructions in the sky before I would move on
something? Well, I guess God felt like I was
dragging my feet, perfectly happy with a Bible
study and children's ministry in the house He
had clearly shown me was meant for more. I
didn't know it, but He was about to do some
skywriting!

Just a few days after the yard sale, a pastor from Williamson, Georgia, called to say, "I
understand you are taking in women."

"Oh, no," I told him hastily. "We hope to
one day in the future, but we are not ready for
that just yet."

He didn't give up that easily. He began to
tell me of a woman in his church who needed

shelter. Her name was Theresa, and she had begun to attend during Vacation Bible School, volunteering right away to work with the children. While helping, she saw something in the lives of some of the children she didn't have, and she wanted it. She asked a member about the joy she saw in them and the worker told her, "That is the love of Jesus in their hearts."

Theresa said she wanted that love in her heart as well, so the workers and the children told her about Jesus. They quoted scripture to her as in John 3:16 – ***"For God so loved the world that He gave His only begotten Son, that whosoever believeth in Him should not perish, but have everlasting life."*** And John 17:3 - ***"And this is life eternal, that they might know Thee the only true God, and Jesus Christ, whom Thou hast sent."*** Theresa was overjoyed to learn God loved her, and Jesus had given His life to provide everlasting life for her. She received Jesus as her Savior, and everyone celebrated, rejoicing with her over her decision to follow Christ.

What the pastor didn't know at the time was Theresa's living situation was a little unusual. Earlier in the year, she had answered an ad in the newspaper to be a live-in housekeeper for a single man, and she was hired. Over time, the relationship grew to be more than employer/employee. They had lived together happily with all the benefits of marriage until she went to church and got saved. That very day, she went home and told him she couldn't live with him anymore because it was not pleasing to God. He got mad and threw her out of the house. Now, she was locked out and looking for a place to live. The pastor said forlornly, "She has no place to go, and we have nowhere to send her."

What went through my head was, "We only have a couch and a nice bedspread we saved from the yard sale." But what came out of my mouth was, "Okay, bring her over. I don't have anyone to stay with her and no food, but we will figure something out."

> "Okay, bring her over. I don't have anyone to stay with her and no food, but we will figure something out."

He said his church would help, and I knew our women would bring in food. Sure enough, every day someone brought leftovers from the previous night's dinner and when all else failed, there was always a tomato sandwich. I mean, during summer in the South, a tomato sandwich is always on the menu!

Theresa had been with us a couple of weeks when her boyfriend, Arthur, called on the office phone and asked to speak to Theresa. He wanted her to come home. "Well," I thought, "here comes trouble. She will go back." But I was wrong.

"No, I'm not coming home," she told him firmly. Then I heard her say, "If you want me to come home, you will have to marry me." Arthur's response was to hang up on her. The next day, he called again and agreed. If that was what it took to get her to come home, he said they would go to Alabama and get married the next day.

"No," she replied. "You need to talk to Pastor Charles at Hanleiter Methodist Church. I've been going there, and if he approves, then we will get married." Again, he hung up angry; but again, he called the next day and agreed. This time he said the magic words. "I will do it because I love you."

The pastor met with Arthur and Theresa and agreed to perform the service. He later commented that under normal circumstances, he would not have agreed to marry a man who was twenty years older than a wife in her thirties, but there was such love between them he thought, "This is right!"

The marriage took place at the house on Poplar Street, with gifts and rice and all the trimmings a loving family of God could provide. It was a marriage made in heaven—two people who took seriously their promise to love each other "until death do us part." The happy couple enjoyed many years together until the Lord called Arthur home. After his death, Theresa came to live with us at the Center to help care for us and we, in turn, cared for her.

Chapter 15

Fishers of Men

*"Follow me and I will make
you fishers of men."*
Matthew 4:19

There is an old adage that says, "When it rains, it pours." Well, God was about to pour out His Spirit to another needy woman, whether or not I was ready, and He didn't wait long to do it.

It happened soon after Theresa came to stay at Hulon House. We were all there cleaning, fellowshipping and praising the Lord—certainly not expecting a crisis involving a gun! Suddenly, a woman from the area shattered our peace and quiet. She ran onto the porch screaming that a man was coming after her with a gun and he was threatening to kill her. It never occurred to any of us we were endangering ourselves by receiving her into the house. She needed help and that is what God had put us there to do, so we were ready to give her whatever protection we could.

"What?!" I yelled. "Get in here, Girl, before we all get killed!" Thankfully, her pursuer did not follow her into our yard. In fact, I never saw him, but I still called the police, and they came to take a report. We gave the woman food and a pallet on the floor in the front room with Theresa. We didn't have any beds to offer them, but they were grateful for the shelter and protection we could provide.

Word of our ministry spread, and women came and went. They seldom stayed long, often returning quickly to the same situation they had run from just a few days earlier. What else could they do? We were a short-term solution, and most could not earn enough money on their own to support themselves and their children.

You have to remember this was the early 1980's, and attitudes toward abused women were different then than they are now. In those days, "society" preferred to look the other way and pretend there was not a problem. Many in Griffin wanted nothing to do with us because we brought the problem they pretended they didn't have to the forefront so it could no longer be denied. But

> "In those days, "society" preferred to look the other way and pretend there was not a problem."

others in the city saw what we were doing and began to respond.

Soon we had twin mattresses on the floors, an old refrigerator became a dresser and boxes were used to store clothing. Even the babies slept in cardboard boxes until some baby beds were donated. We did whatever it took to provide shelter, food, and a safe place for those who came to us. Of course, we told them about Christ and fellowshipped with them as long as we could before going home to our husbands and families.

That became our pattern as women rotated through the house. In the mornings, we would check with them as soon as our husbands left for work and the kids were in school. We didn't have cell phones, so it was clean our homes quick, quick, quick, and hurry down to Poplar Street to make sure everyone was still in one piece. I'm not sure how we avoided getting into trouble with the men involved with our residents. We were so ignorant of whose homes we were going into to get the women out, or even which ones might have guns or knives, but we had the boldness of the Lord for sure!

As life at Hulon House ebbed and flowed from day to day, we moved along with the ministry. Some days, I was happy and obedient to this call of God on my life. Other days, I would throw up my hands and go home, asking, "Lord, why am I doing this?" But always, I felt that steady pull, drawing me back to the knowledge I was supposed to "fish" for God. Our core Bible study group believed in that call right along with me. We were reading Scripture together and reminding each other of what the Word of God said. If something was broken, we laid hands on it and prayed for healing—be it human, animal or mechanical.

> *"If something was broken, we laid hands on it and prayed for healing—be it human, animal or mechanical."*

We prayed for people, horses, goats, dogs, cats, cars—anything that needed a touch from God. We took God at His word and saw miracles happen. We watched in awe as He fulfilled His promises, meeting our needs on a daily basis.

Walking with God in that realm is exciting. It's a whole other place. I can't explain it and even if I could, you wouldn't understand it unless you have walked there. One thing I know: it is worth giving up everything for that space! And yet, it is not so much a giving up as a following after. At last, I understood the feelings of Simon Peter and Andrew, his brother, along with James and his brother, John. When

Jesus walked along the shores of the Sea of Galilee and called them to become fishers of men, they immediately dropped their nets and followed Him. We women had homes, husbands, and children, but we were following after Jesus because He said, "Come, follow me." And so, we boldly and fearlessly followed the Master, facing whatever trouble the women brought in with them, yet covered always by His grace.

Chapter 16

No Room in the Inn

*Come unto me, all ye that labour and are
heavy laden, and I will give you rest.*
Matthew 11:28

Knowing you are in the center of God's will
is a wonderful experience, but it is not always
an easy place to be. That truth became infi-
nitely clearer to me as the days passed. Every
few days, one of those "problems that Griffin
didn't have" showed up on our doorsteps looking for a safe harbor. We didn't turn anyone
away, but our two little apartments were full to
the max.

"Lord," I begged, "tell me where to put all
these women!" His answer led me back to my
Board of Directors. So off I went to ask for approval to rent the upstairs. Thank goodness
those Directors were men and women of prayer
who walked in faith and believed in God. They
saw my request as a move of His Spirit, and
they were willing to go with Him into the un-
known. None of us knew where the additional
rent money would come from, but we did know

that if God was leading, and we believed He was, then He would provide.

When I left the Board meeting that night, we had approval to rent the whole house! What a joy to serve with a Board who had spiritual eyes to see and feet to serve because they all put feet to their prayers. Everywhere they went in their day-to-day lives, they spoke about our ministry and our needs. Thanks, in a large part, to the efforts of our Board of Directors, we began to feel like the city was covering us with a big umbrella of love and prayer.

I knew how much we needed all that love and all those prayers, but I also knew the reality of living where the rubber meets the road. We now had an entire house full of women with all the problems a house full of women can bring. They came from all walks of life with all kinds of issues: victims of abuse, drug addicts, alcoholics, and the homeless. All were on a downward spiral and looking for just a tiny ray of hope life could get better. We just loved them, told them about

> "We just loved them, told them about Jesus, and helped them get to the right agencies in Griffin."

Jesus, and helped them get to the right agencies in Griffin.

We also tried to teach a few rules to help them move from the streets to polite society because many of them came from backgrounds that could only be described as "anything goes." One day, I came to the house on wash day. Shirts, pants, dresses and underwear were hanging from the front and top porch rails and all over the bushes in the front yard. I had a royal hissy fit!! In case you were wondering, that's southern-speak for stomping around and yelling a lot.

"You can't do that," I ranted. "We are not a wash house down in the boonies. (More southern-speak for so far in the backwoods no one can find you.) We are a ministry in town!"

"Well, how do we dry the clothes?" they wanted to know.

It was a logical, legitimate question, so off I went on another trip. This time, I headed to the hardware store to get some wire to make a clothesline in the back yard. Inventory was increasing, and so were the rules, which now included "no clothing hanging from the porch rails."

Each day brought new challenges. On one occasion, I watched a young, inexperienced mother pick up a half-full bottle of milk that

had been sitting out on the counter all night
and hand it to her baby. Another hissy fit was
about to break out, but I calmed down quickly
when it became clear she really had no idea
what she had done wrong.

It didn't take long for me to see we needed
house rules and a live-in house mother to
watch over our ladies. That realization led me
back to Christy Cleghorn. I introduced you to
Christy in Chapter 4 as the one who got me
involved in counseling with her friends at the
emergency room. Christy was a helper and, of
course, we had put her right to work as a volunteer at the house. We were glad to get
someone who was so compassionate for the
work we were doing. She loved helping women
and children and had an especially soft spot
for the babies.

An old white truck that belonged to her
mother was Christy's rescue wagon, and she
used it to save anyone she knew who was
hurting or in danger. She not only told women
about the ministry, she also provided trans-
portation to haul them out of harm's way. She
drove that truck like a maniac when she was
bringing someone to safety. You could hear her
coming well before she came into view, and we
all expected the nuts and bolts to fall out in

the street any minute, but somehow God held it together.

Christy loved and knew how to care for the women. She would talk to them and settle them down after a bad night with an abuser. If need be, she would stay awake with one of them all night, listening and comforting. She was so good with the residents that I went to the Board and asked if she could come live at the house to be the manager. There would be no pay, of course, because we had no money to give her. They readily agreed, and oddly enough, so did she!

> *"We were still a very small ministry and I felt we just needed to do the work as to the Lord."*

There was no job description to give Christy because I didn't know what that was until James Johnston, President of the Board at that time, showed me what we needed. I fought him over writing down descriptions for each position. We were still a very small ministry and I felt we just needed to do the work **"as to the Lord"** (Colossians 3:23) like we had been doing all along. James saw things differently and taught me that a job with no job description is like life with no goals. Without written guidelines to tell employees or volunteers what they should be doing, they have no way to know whether or not they are meeting expectations. The accountability provided by a job description helped people do a good job. It took me a while to see the light, but when I did, I was grateful for the good advice James gave me.

Chapter 17
Profiles of Courage

*Wherefore take unto you the whole
armour of God, that ye may be
able to withstand in the evil day,
and having done all, to stand.*
Ephesians 6:13

Finally, we felt like we were uptown for
sure because we now had a Resident Manager
in the house, which took a lot of responsibility
off of the Bible study group. I know it seems
crazy to have a person with a drug problem
oversee a bunch of women, some of whom had
drug problems, but somehow the combination
worked. I taught Christy about the Lord, Personal Growth (a program in Griffin) taught her
how to get free of drugs, and they all taught
me about street ministry. Christy understood
the women in ways I could not, and together,
we helped them become strong and take a
stand against the oppression in their lives.

As I watched the women come and go, I often saw myself in them and yearned for them
to understand the grace and mercy of God that
I had found in Christ Jesus. I loved seeing the

changes in their lives, even if it was just a little every day. It was wonderful to observe them as they grew strong enough to leave captivity behind for good. On one occasion, a normally timid resident decided to go back to her home for her "good nightgowns" she was not allowed to have when she left. To me, it appeared to be an unnecessary fight.

"No," I told her. "A few gowns are not worth that much trouble."

She disagreed strongly and thought it was time to take a stand for the good things in her life. I began to see it was not so much the clothing, but the belief in her ability to escape her former life that was at stake and finally agreed she should go. We got the police to accompany her, and she was able to get from her old home what belonged to her. She had learned in Scripture she could overcome the obstacles Satan had erected in her life, and God would supply the armor she would need to stand her ground. That is exactly what she did. What a woman!

Then there was Trish, another resident who eventually discovered an inner strength she did not know she possessed. Early in 1984, she came into the house with two precious little ones, seeking protection from her abusive husband. Trish swears there were no rules in the house until she arrived, and then we made up all of them because of her. We have never been able to convince her otherwise.

Because she was throwing up constantly, Christy insisted Trish take a pregnancy test, and sure enough, the test was positive. What an unexpected and unplanned development! A baby often binds the mother to her abuser even tighter because supporting herself and her children without his income is extremely difficult. In the meantime, Trish's husband was making big promises: he would stop all his partying, and more importantly, he would stop hitting her. As often happens, Trish believed his lies, and after being at the Center for only a month, she went back to her husband. Many abused women who escape will later return to the same situation. They desperately want to believe the husband will change because the alternative of trying to provide for the family alone is overwhelming and frightening.

> *"Many abused women who escape will later return to the same situation because the alternative of trying to provide for the family alone is overwhelming and frightening."*

The changes Trish's husband promised never happened, and six months into her pregnancy, she came back to the Christian Women's Center with only the clothes on her back. The other residents shared their clothing with her, and Brenda Hooper, who was totally captivated by Trish's little red-headed angel, went out and bought clothes for her babies. This time, Trish found the strength to make the break permanent, and the little family stayed at the Center for about another six months as she struggled to get on her feet. Finally, early in May of 1985, there was a happy announcement in the minutes of the Board of Directors meeting that Trish had left the Christian Women's Center because she had found a job and rented an apartment.

Trish did return to the Center in 2002, but this time as an employee. She says that during the ensuing four years, she worked every position there was except for Executive Director and bookkeeper. Wherever there was a need, Trish was willing to fill it. She even remembers a time when money was so tight that she and another employee quit their jobs and became volunteers in order to keep the doors open.

Such times always drove all of us to our knees before God. He always responded just in the nick of time to keep the ministry alive to help women like Trish escape from the bondage of abuse or any other crisis they might be facing. When asked to describe that time in her life, Trish's answer is evidence that leaving the kind of trauma she endured is not an easy process. She simply says, "I am one of those who got out, got help, and continue to go forward in life daily." Trish remains a precious Christian and friend to this day.

About the time Trish was getting her world in order, Mellodie's life was falling apart. She had been raised in a blended family with issues so severe that to call them dysfunctional could have been considered a compliment. Mellodie wanted her life to be different, and was determined to escape the bonds of abuse, drugs, and alcohol that entangled her family so securely. She dedicated herself to completing high school and continuing on to college and was the only one of her siblings to do so.

At a young age, Mellodie had received Jesus as her Savior and spent hours studying the scriptures, looking for answers to the emptiness, misery, and pain in her life. She attended church regularly, but unfortunately, over time her understanding of Jesus evolved into a set of rules for the Christian life that she could never quite live up to. It was an elusive standard she had set for herself, and the inability to attain what she thought God required eventually caused her to give up the battle.

The circumstances of Mellodie's early family life and her heart's desire to follow Christ created a war inside her that manifested in depression, psychic dissociation, drug abuse, and suicidal tendencies. Unable to find help even from psychiatrists, Mellodie made a series of bad choices that led her further into the kind of lifestyle she had so desperately wanted to avoid as a child.

Finally, in 1985, the downward spiral had drawn her into an abusive relationship, intravenous drug use, and slum-like living conditions for her and her two children. She knew she needed to escape; indeed, she says God told her to leave, and He would take care of her. However, as is often the case with abused women, fear kept her in the situation: her partner had vowed to kill her if she left. Again, she heard God speak to her about leaving, and this time she found the courage to obey. After two unsuccessful attempts to flee, Mellodie and her children managed to reach the safety of the Christian Women's Center.

I will let Mellodie tell you how her story ends in her own words: "At the door to the Center, before anyone answered, I told God, 'This is it. If this doesn't work, I'm done. I will throw myself in front of a moving semi-truck before I return to the life I just left.' The rest of the story is a miracle. At the Center, I found acceptance, I found love, I found scriptural teaching, and finally, I found GRACE.

> "At the Center, I found acceptance, I found love, I found scriptural teaching, and finally, I found GRACE."

I had never understood that God was not expecting me to be perfect. He knew I could not follow His rules, so He had provided a way. Jesus died, covered me with His blood, and redeemed my life, soul, and spirit. I received the gift of the Holy Spirit to guide and help me. I have never returned to the life I led before.

For 35 years, I have been celibate and drug free. I continued to battle with depression for many years before God finally delivered me from that as well. For those who say God doesn't exist, I reply they should look at my life. Through the grace of God, I am free, and my children are God-fearing, productive adults who love the Lord and have a relationship with Him."

What can be said about women such as
these, who endured adversity of this kind with
such great courage? Breaking away is not
easy! One statistic in an online article indi-
cates that some women will return to their
abusers as many as seven times before they
are able to leave for good. Both physical and
emotional barriers must be overcome before
the victim can break away permanently. Not
everyone possesses the mental and physical
stamina to make leaving a reality in their lives.
We need to admire and encourage all women
who display the strength and fortitude it takes
to come out of their situations and take a
stand against abuse in any form, in any place,
and at any time!

Chapter 18

Looking for the Open Door

For which of you, intending to build a tower,
sitteth not down first and counteth the
the cost, whether he have
sufficient to finish it?
Luke 14:28

Walking with God is like no other walk, and hearing Him speak is one of the greatest "highs" a person can experience on this earth. Any child of God desires to have that experience, but with the hearing of God's voice comes a demand from Him that we move in response. The choice is ours to make. We can put it off for a minute or a year, but we know deep down where the Spirit of God groans we need to move toward Him. We understand there will be a cost, but the Bible says in Deuteronomy 31:8, ***"He will not fail thee, neither forsake thee."*** I was glad of that promise because the cost for me was steadily growing. Not only was the ministry taking time away from my home and family, but God was stretching and growing me in ways I had never imagined and didn't always find comfortable.

There was about to be another price-hike in the cost of this "fishing" expedition God had me on, and had I known what was coming, I would probably have run in the other direction. It started with a visit to Hulon House by the Fire Marshall. He told me that if we had a fire, the stairwell would act like a chimney, drawing the flames and smoke upward. Anyone unfortunate enough to be on the upper floor would be trapped. To continue to occupy the house, we would have to provide another way for the women and children to escape in case of a fire. Of course, remodeling a building that old would take lots of money, and because we had none, our only option was to move.

After the Fire Marshall left, I went looking for an open church in which to pray. Many churches were now locking their doors during the day because of a recent rash of thefts, but the doors at First Baptist Church of Griffin were always open, and I headed to its altar. All afternoon, I stayed at that altar telling the Lord how we needed another building. I also suggested we needed a plan of how to get that building and asked if He would please show me where it was located. Relieved the problem now belonged to God, I went back to watch and wait for the open door to the larger building I had asked for.

"Wait" is the key word here because having the patience to wait for God to move is hard and takes a lot of endurance. He often holds back on an answer to see if we will really wait for Him to do the job or if we will get impatient and try to do it for Him. I have jumped in many a time to help Him out and got caught with my hand in the cookie jar. But this time, it had to be God because no one associated with the ministry could accomplish this huge need on our own. We just had to have faith He would come through. So, we waited.

> "Relieved that the problem now belonged to God, I went back to watch and wait for the open door."

During that time, we discussed and agreed on what was needed in a new location. We wanted a building that was all on one level, a kitchen where a mother could cook while watching her children playing on playground equipment outside, and a big oak tree in the yard for the little ones to play under and stay cool in the summer. Most of all, it had to be a safe place for the staff, women, and children.

I began to look at places available in the Griffin area that were for sale and even some that were not, but nothing seemed to fit our requirements. Then a faithful member of our study group, Mace Palmer, told me of a building in Sunnyside, Georgia, that was for sale, and she wanted to show it to me. I didn't even bother to pray because I knew Sunnyside was too far out in the country for the county sheriff to provide timely protection. We needed to be in the city, close enough for the police to reach us quickly if a dangerous situation should develop with one of the residents. I continued searching for a building in and around Griffin. I just knew it was there; all I had to do was find it, and I needed to find it quickly. I was getting desperate for a place that would house all the women. I knew there was a limit on how long the Fire Marshall would wait before he shut us down.

It's funny how sometimes you think you are waiting on God, but in actuality you are just putting together your own plan. I'm sure God was laughing at me because I had my hand in the cookie jar again. I was trying so hard to help Him find that building and I had to exhaust everything in Griffin before I reluctantly admitted the open door just might be in Sunnyside. I called Mace and asked to go see the building. She couldn't go that day but was able to arrange for Brenda and me to meet with the realtor and the owner of the building.

Mace said the building once was home to the Sunnyside School. I knew of the building because my father had told me tales of going to school there as a boy. Isn't that just like God? First, He gave us a house where Hulons had once lived and now we were looking at a building where my daddy had played in the yard and drew water from the well.

As Brenda and I toured the property with the owner, Mr. Johnny Ward, we were amazed at how it met all of the criteria we wanted for the women and children. There was even playground equipment in the yard with an oak tree nearby! Brenda and I chattered like magpies about where things could go inside the building and asked at least a hundred questions. I'm sure Mr. Ward thought we were crazy ladies, but he answered all our questions with quiet respect.

In this property, God had provided everything we had asked for, but that fact went right over my head. I was still convinced this was not the place for us. On the way back to Griffin, I kept saying to Brenda that surely God did not want us so far out from town. How would the women get to us? How long would it take the sheriff to respond to a call? Not only that, the realtor had told us a Day Care Center actually had a contract on the property, and it appeared it would go through; but if anything went awry, we would have first chance at the building. Even if that contract did fall through, Mr. Ward was asking for a lot of money, which we didn't have, nor any idea where to get any. What we did have was faith in our work with the women and children, faith God was ready to move us somewhere, and faith He would provide.

As we drove back from Sunnyside, I was determined to keep looking in Griffin to see if we had missed anything. I did believe we would have a new building, although most people would question the logic of that belief. If we couldn't even afford to add a fire escape to the house we currently occupied, how in the world would we be able to buy a building and land? I didn't know, but

> "I focused on Jesus' words in Matthew 8:13: **"Go thy way; and as thou hast believed, so be it done unto thee."**

I just knew it would happen, so I focused on Jesus' words in Matthew 8:13: **"Go thy way; and as thou hast believed, so be it done unto thee."** All I needed to do was to stay at peace and wait on the Lord to show me the open door when He was ready to open it. Of course, I was quite sure it would be in Griffin!

Chapter 19

Walking Through the Door

*Be strong and of good courage, and
do it: fear not, nor be dismayed:
for the Lord God, even my
God, will be with thee.*
1 Chronicles 28:20

A few months prior to my visit to Sunnyside, the Board of Directors had voted to incorporate the ministry and a new name was selected. Not long after that, the Griffin Daily News published an article on the ministry of the Christian Women's Center (the new name), which was operating from a house on Poplar Street in Griffin. The resulting influx of women put such a strain on our limited space that even I could see God forcing me to abandon my search within the city and seriously consider the Sunnyside location.

In the meantime, we got word the Day Care's contract on the property had fallen through, and it was on the market again. It was obvious to all of us God was at work. With the Board's approval, the search began for a bank willing to loan money to a fledgling ministry. After being turned down by several different places, I made an appointment with a loan officer in a local bank who was familiar with our ministry because his wife was working with us as a volunteer. I was hoping she might have a little influence in tipping the scales our way, but it didn't work. I ran into another brick wall.

Looking at the payment that would be due each month, the cost of utilities and the expense required to feed the number of women we were housing, it was obvious from a business standpoint we would have a difficult time meeting those requirements. Even though he was a Christian, the loan officer could not see how we could manage, given the meager amount of donations coming in each month. He looked at me and said, "I cannot give you the money, Sue, because this town will turn on me and shut me down when you default, and I have to close your doors."

As I stood to leave, I looked at him across the desk and said firmly and confidently, "Thank you for your time. I understand your reservations as a businessman, but let me assure you this purchase is ordained by God, and He will provide the money. If not through you, then someone else will get the blessing because they are willing to partner with us."

Although I left his office with my head held high, in my heart I was on my knees before God. "What now?" I asked Him. "I'm at the end of my rope."

> "Although I left his office with my head held high, in my heart I was on my knees before God."

Of course, that is exactly where He wanted me to be. His answer in the recesses of my heart was not what I wanted to hear. "Just wait on Me."

This time, the wait was shorter. We had all reached the point of total dependence on God, and He was ready to move. Three days after the meeting at the bank, the officer called me to say they would loan us the money. Only God could have produced that change of heart, and we all knew it.

We placed a contract on the new property and set a time and date for the closing. We always had needs to pray over, but this one was BIG: we had to raise $5,000 in one week for earnest money and $15,000 in the second week for the down payment at closing. At the same time, all the normal expenses at Hulon House still had to be met until we could close the deal and move.

Now God REALLY began to test our faith. The day of the closing arrived, and we still did not have all the money for the down payment. As the appointed time inched closer, our prayers got stronger. Finally, just one hour before the closing, the final $1,000 came in from one of the mills in town and we rejoiced in God's goodness.

Three corporate officers attended the closing: President, Sue Hulon (that's me); Treasurer, Suan Hunt; and Secretary, Martha Rawdin. We stopped on the sidewalk near the offices to pray, but I decided we needed to pray in the meeting before it began. Martha stated later she had no qualms about praying outside, but to ask that group of businessmen and women if we could pray inside was intimidating. She says she marveled at the boldness she saw as I looked around the table at all those realtors, lawyers, and bank representatives and asked sweetly if anyone would object if we began the meeting with prayer. What could they say? Of course, no one objected!

We prayed, and God showed up. We know He was there because at the end of the meeting, both realtors and the surveyor endorsed their checks and handed them back to Suan. Even the seller made a contribution to help us purchase his own property! In case you were wondering, the answer is YES, we certainly do serve an AMAZING God!

When I consider those days and what God accomplished through all of us, I have to agree with Martha. It did take a lot of courage and determination to meet the challenges we faced, and somehow God infused those qualities into me. He took me from having a violent fear of speaking in public to a place of such confidence that I could face rebellious women, angry husbands, disgruntled contributors, or even bankers and lawyers, speaking His truth boldly and without hesitation. That boldness, my friends, is a miracle if I ever saw one.

> *"In case you were wondering, the answer is YES, we certainly do serve an AMAZING God!"*

Chapter 20

The Valley of Dry Bones

And (I) shall put my Spirit in you, and
ye shall live, and I shall place
you in your own land.
Ezekiel 37:14

The Book of John in the New Testament of the Bible tells of the Apostle John's three-year walk with Jesus and shares insights on the beginning struggles of the infant church. Then, he ends his Gospel with this statement: ***"And there are also many other things which Jesus did, the which, if they should be written every one, I suppose that even the world itself could not contain the books that should be written. Amen."*** (John 21:25)

That sentiment is exactly how I feel about this book relating the beginning of the Christian Women's Center. My original intent was to include many more stories of the women whose lives were changed because there was a place of refuge where the Word of God was instilled in their hearts, but how could I leave out any of the precious people who passed through our doors? Yet, there is no way to include them all. The book would be too large to lift!

Suffice it to say that we did move the ministry to the Sunnyside location in July, 1984. Twenty-five years later, I retired from my position as Executive Director, but the Christian Women's Center is still open and functioning in the same location all of these years after moving there. What a testimony to God's faithfulness to "the least of these."

So many milestones occurred during my time with the Center:

Marriages took place.

Families were restored.

Babies were born.

Federal funding was obtained and lost because of our stand for Jesus.

United Way funding was obtained and lost for the same reason.

I finally became a salaried employee rather than a volunteer. Additionally, we eventually hired a secretary, a shelter director, a training program director, a nursery director, and a bookkeeper.

A Thrift Store was begun with proceeds from the sale of donated clothing and household goods going to support the Center's needs.

Disunity arose in the Board of Directors over whether to remove the word "Christian" from our name so we could obtain federal funding again. The membership of the corporation stood strong against that move, and two-thirds of the Board resigned. However, we found others whose hearts matched ours and marched on.

Vehicles were purchased along the way, and vehicles died. Somehow, through God's grace, we always managed to come up with another one.

We began and supported a house for needy women in Ukraine.

We began and supported a branch of the Christian Women's Center in Piedmont, Alabama.

We built a large nursery behind the original building to house our children and nursery workers. We almost went broke doing this project because donors gave their budget donations to the nursery fund, but we came through it intact with a wonderful place for the children to play and learn about Jesus.

The Thrift Store became too small and was moved to a store that quadrupled the first, both in size and rent. How did we afford that kind of increase? Only God!

All of these and many other happenings were important and chronicle how the ministry changed and grew over the years, but what is really important is what happened in the hearts of the women who came into the program. One day, I was reading in Chapter Thirty-seven of Ezekiel, where the Prophet tells of a conversation he had with God about a valley of dry bones. Of course, Ezekiel and God are discussing Israel, but that discussion also reminded me of the changes the Word of God brought about for the residents of the CWC. In my mind, it was as if God were speaking to me rather than Ezekiel.

> "We told them about Jesus, we read the Word to them, and we spoke the Word around them."

"And He said unto me...can these bones live?" Is there any hope for these women and children?

"O, Lord God, thou knowest." Only you know the answer to that, Lord. I know nothing of their world and not enough of Yours.

"Again He said unto me, Prophesy upon these bones, and say unto them, O ye dry bones, hear the Word of the Lord." So that is what we did. Every woman and child who came into the Center received the Word of the Lord directly from the Bible. We told them about Jesus, we read the Word to them, and we spoke the Word around them. As they began to hear Scripture in lessons taught during the day and read it in personal study at night, we could see God putting their lives back together.

"As I prophesied, there was a noise, and behold a shaking, and the bones came together, bone to his bone." We could see them struggle to stand on their feet as God's Word spoke hope into their hearts. They had a desire to leave the death and dryness of the valley and move into life. But it was a hard time because there were no tendons or flesh to hold them together, only God.

"And when I beheld, lo, the sinews and the flesh came up upon them, and the skin covered them above: but there was no breath in them." They had begun to change for the better. There was a fresh, new look on their faces, and more self-assurance in their walk. The drugs were out, and healthy eating and sleeping habits were in, giving them an I-think-I'm-going-to-make-it attitude. Yet something was missing, and that something was a commitment to the Word they had been receiving.

This was a very fragile time in their lives, and it was the point where we lost a lot of women from the program. They looked good, felt good, and wanted control of their lives again. They began to wonder what they were doing in a program like ours. Often, the family and friends agreed with them and encouraged them to come home. What they didn't realize was that the body had been repaired, but it was God holding the bones together, protecting and caring for them. When they left the program, they found out life was too hard without Him. They got angry because everything they had learned at the Center seemed false, hope was lost again, and they quickly fell back into old lifestyles.

"Then said he unto me, prophesy...and say to the wind, Thus saith the Lord God; Come from the four winds, O breath, and breathe upon these slain, that they may live. So I prophesied as he commanded me, and the breath came into them, and they lived, and stood up upon their feet, an exceeding great army." Ahhhh, but the ones who stayed! We continued to give them the Word of the Lord more and more until the breath came into them, and they stood on their own. We saw them begin to take responsibility for their lives before God, both the good and the bad. They began to speak the Word to others because they had the breath of life in

them. They began to follow Jesus and be a witness of what He had done in their lives. They had become a part of the vast army of God.

"Behold, they say, Our bones are dried, and our hope is lost... Therefore prophesy and say unto them, Thus saith the Lord God; Behold, O My people, I will...cause you to come up out of your graves." No more did these women say, "We have no hope, our hope is gone, we are cut off and put in this place." Their graves had been opened and God had brought them up and into life.

> *"Their graves had been opened and God had brought them up and into life."*

"And (I) shall put My Spirit in you, and ye shall live, and I shall place you in your own land." That is just exactly what God did for the women who came through the Christian Women's Center as they followed Him. His Spirit resided within them to guide their lives, and He settled them in their own land, a land where they were to witness to the Word of the Lord, to His healing power, and to how He had called them forth out of the valley of death and dry bones into a full life with Jesus Christ.

Chapter 21

The Army of God

*For though we walk in the flesh, we do not war
after the flesh: for the weapons of our warfare
are not carnal, but mighty through God
to the pulling down of strong holds.*
2 Corinthians 10:3-4

As I come now to the end of this writing, I find it difficult to bring the story to a close. Documenting God's heart for hurting women and children has been a true labor of love. At the same time, putting it all on paper has been one of the most difficult things I have ever done. The process has brought back many wonderful memories, but also others that are best forgotten.

As I consider what God accomplished with a few women in a small town in Georgia, I am filled with wonder. We were untrained and had no particular skills to qualify us for such a ministry, but like good soldiers, we just made ourselves available when the General called. That analogy makes me think of a story I once heard along those same lines.

During a time of war, there was a young man who believed so strongly in his country that he joined the Army. He went to boot camp where an intake officer arranged for him to have a haircut and a uniform so he could look the part. Every day he trained for war, read all the manuals required, and did the war exercises with enthusiasm. His hard work was noted, and he even received a special commendation for his performance. Then came the day he had waited and trained for - the call to be shipped out. To say he was excited would have been an understatement.

> "As I consider what God accomplished with a few women in a small town in Georgia, I am filled with wonder."

"I'm actually going to war," he thought to himself. "I will finally be able to fight for my country."

A few short weeks later, he was transported to the front lines, and it was a different story from what he had expected. He could see, feel, and smell death everywhere. This was not like the war games they had played at basic training. He made it to the foxhole, but when the order came to move out, HE FROZE. All around him, members of his unit were

dying as they bravely left the safety of the fox-
holes. To his horror, he even watched his captain stumble and fall to enemy fire.

"I'll just stay here in this foxhole," he
mumbled to himself. "I'm not going any further."

Just then, a message arrived from the
commanding general. "Your captain is dead.
Because of your performance in boot camp,
you are receiving a field commission. You are
the captain now. Lead your men out, take the
land and hold."

No officer training, no directions, just a
commission: take the land. After the war, a
reporter remarked, "You must have had good
training to hold out for so long."

The young captain replied, "No, I'm just a
foot soldier the general called out to do a job."

That's exactly how I felt when God called
me into ministry to women. I was in the army,
to be sure, but living in the safety of boot camp
and playing war games. I and the women who
met with me for Bible study every Thursday
were totally oblivious to the spiritual warfare
going on all around us. We were diligently
learning the Word and applying it to our lives.
We believed God meant what He said and
prayed over everybody and everything.
Miracles happened and it was fun to see the

glory of God working, but we were like children
with a gun. A gun can be fun to shoot, but we
didn't know the true power of it, the danger in
using it, or the responsibility that comes with
owning such a weapon. We were just kids in
the spiritual realm—kids at boot camp going
through the motions of war.

Then, God gave the vision and with it the
call to move into enemy territory. The house
opened, and the women and children came.
Oh, the hurt, poor in spirit, poor in the physical, poor in worldly possessions—they were so
WOUNDED. Spiritual death was all around; we
could smell it. We could see it in their eyes and
in their words. The Word of God says Satan
comes to steal, kill, and destroy, but Jesus
comes to give abundant life. We struggled daily
to break the cycle of death and destruction
and show them the life Jesus offered.

I was in the foxhole then and couldn't go
back. The transport of innocence had dropped
me off at the front lines to engage the enemy,
and the battle had begun. I could see the dead
and dying all around me in the form of hurting
women, little children.

"Where is the captain? Where is the
church? I NEED TO GO HOME! I don't like
seeing these people in pain. I'm not cut out for
this job! Oh, God, how did I get here? Just let

me go back to my children and husband, back to innocence. I won't tell anyone I saw the hurting people."

But the General replied, "Someone's got to lead them out, or there will be more losses." He guaranteed me He would provide all the power I needed if I would just move in obedience. I took Him at His word, and you have now read how God orchestrated the fulfillment of His plan.

Eventually, that plan grew into a great responsibility. We had a twenty-one-member Board of Directors, fifteen staff members needing salaries, and three programs being operated: a short-term shelter for women in immediate crisis, a one-year training program for those who were ready to turn their lives around, and a 7,800 square-foot thrift store with approximately $45,000 worth of merchandise. Budget-wise, we went from a few receipts in a cigar box to around $200,000 per year. More important than those numbers were the successes in the lives of the women. Addictions were being overcome, strongholds were being broken, and souls were being saved.

But as the victories came, so did the battles. Just as in war, the enemy began to take notice of our advancements. He hid land mines in strategic places in an effort to destroy God's plan. We faced explosive financial difficulties: $65,000 of federal funding support was withdrawn. Later, $10,000 of United Way support was also lost; yet in the face of financial chaos, God provided. He just sent more believers to give or called on current supporters to give more. At a time when we should have gone under, God took care of the deficit and allowed the second phase of our nursery building to be completed. How could that happen? The power of the Father, that's how. He knew who had His money.

The second bomb went off: explosive relationships. We had to deal with condemnation from some areas in the community because of the Center's stand with Christ. It's hard to live in the world and follow the Word, but we did it then, and we must do it now. Joshua 24:15 says in part: **"Choose you this day whom ye will serve...but as for me and my house, we will serve the Lord."** It's a daily choice, and when we choose God, He is always faithful.

> "It's hard to live in the world and follow the Word, but we did it then, and we must do it now."

So, we took the hill and counted our losses. Programs, like limbs, had been blown away. We had to regroup and decide whether to go forward to the next hill or turn back. Of course, we already knew the answer. We had sung about it way back in the beginning: "I have decided to follow Jesus; no turning back, no turning back."

Now, Dear Reader, we have come to the end of this tale of how the Christian Women's Center came into being. Someone else will have to write the stories of the women who passed through our doors, "the rest of the story" as radio commentator Paul Harvey used to say. As for me, Jesus has prepared a place for me, and I fully expect He will be coming to receive me unto Himself in the not-too-distant future. In the meantime, I have the peace of knowing my eternal future is secure. My question to you is, "Do you have that kind of peace?"

If you know Jesus personally, I will see you one day in heaven. If you don't have a relationship with Him already, you can. He's waiting patiently for you to move in His direction. Get a Bible, read the Book of John, and get to know **"the Lamb of God, which taketh away the sin of the world."** (John 1:29) Then look me up one day in the Promised Land!

On September 20, 2020, Mary Sue Hulon-Palmer joined her husband and parents in eternity as she slipped peacefully into the presence of her Lord and Savior, Jesus Christ. I am quite sure there was great rejoicing over her arrival in heaven, but here on earth, we are having a hard time letting her go. Sue was such a powerful presence in our lives for so many years, the process of living without her has proven to be difficult for family and friends alike.

About two weeks before her death, Sue told me she felt as if she had done too little in her life with the opportunities she was given. I disagreed with her heartily and reminded her of how many people she had affected positively through her church and the many community organizations through which she served.

Her honors and awards included Woman of the Year and Woman of Achievement for her service to the community through the Christian Women's Center. Sue was a prolific writer and some of her many stories are published in a book entitled "Living Out Loud with Family, Friends and the Farm."

The accomplishment most dear to Sue's heart was the Christian Women's Center. She was the founder and Executive Director, as well as a member of the Board of Directors for twenty-five years. Records compiled at the Center from 1983 through 1996 indicate 2,056 women and 1,749 children received food and shelter during that time. I have no idea how many others were helped in the remaining twelve years Sue was active in the ministry or in the twelve years since she retired. Suffice it to say that many families were touched by her commitment to following God's call on her life.

The fondest wish of Sue's later life was to complete this book on the miraculous origins of the Center she loved so dearly. The original plan was to include many stories of the lost daughters who discovered their true identity through the love of Christ, but Sue's declining health required us to limit the story to only the first two years of the Center's history.

The fondest wish of my life has been to place a copy of this book in Sue's hands before she took her seat in the heavenlies with Jesus. Sadly, it was not meant to be. However, those of us who loved her then and love her still have persevered, and the story has now been told. Even though she is not present at this time, I

know she is as pleased as I that you now hold
the finished product in your hands.

Charlotte Davis

The Journey...

Bible Study at
the Farm before
the Vision

A Few of the Study
Group with the New
Yard Sign

The First Bible
Study at Hulon
House

Hulon House in
the Big, March
Snow

Sue Hulon

Foot Washing at the
Maundy Thursday
Service on 3/31/83

Cooking Lesson
at Hulon House

Caring for the
Children

The Kitchen Gets an Overhaul.

The Kitchen
Doubles as a
Bedroom

Overcrowded
Conditions

Working on
Griffin's Longest
Honey-do List

It's Official!
New Name,
New
Charter –
11/30/83

The Property on
School Road,
Sunnyside, GA

Announcing Our
Presence in the
Community

Extending a
Helping Hand to
Someone in Need

More Books from Greentree Publishers

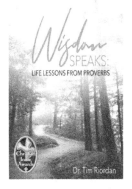

Wisdom Speaks: Life Lessons from Proverbs

By Tim Riordan

Have you ever wished for a "How To" book on life? God has given us one in the book of Proverbs. Join pastor and Bible teacher Dr. Tim Riordan on a journey through this book of wisdom where you study one of the most read books of the Bible.

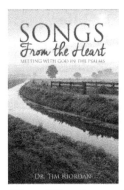

Songs from the Heart: Meeting with God in the Psalms

By Tim Riordan

Songs from the Heart: Meeting with God in the Psalms is a Bible study/ devotional on the beloved book of Psalms. Dr. Tim Riordan shares insights, Bible teaching, and storytelling, making personal application to your life. Chosen as book of the year in Bible study and theology in 2016 By Christian Small Publishers Association.

Greentreepublishers.com

When God Promises

Taking God at His Word will free you from Worry, Stress, & Fear

By Julie McCoy

This six-week study draws on the experiences of people in the Bible who discovered the power of taking God at His word. As you explore their stories you will learn how trusting God's faithfulness to do what He says will give you victory over worry, stress, and fear.

Reaching for Life

By Victoria Teague

with Connie Singleton

Following an eleven-year cocaine addiction and a dangerous career as a dancer in the sex industry, Victoria Teague built a new life on top of her secrets. For ten years, post-recovery, she sat in the pews of her church with a grateful heart and a "zip-locked" mouth. Only a precious, trusted few (among them her husband and the woman who led her to Jesus Christ) knew her complete, spiritual rags-to-riches story.

Greentreepublishers.com

Made in the USA
Monee, IL
02 September 2021

76205354R00089